TOURISM SCENE IN NEPAL

TOURISM SCENE IN NEPAL

Yajna Raj Satyal

ADROIT PUBLISHERS
NEW DELHI

Tourism Scene in Nepal

First Published, 2000

ISBN 81-87392-05-3

Published by:
ADROIT PUBLISHERS
C-8/2, Yamuna Vihar,
Delhi-110053

Typesetting by:
Stylish Laser Typesetter
Delhi - 110053

Printed at:
Efficient Offset Press
Shahzada Bagh, New Delhi-110035

FOREWORD

Keeping in view of the International Tourism which is a large and steadily expanding industry, Nepal has been playing a tremendous receptive part for the development of tourism in the country. She has the most favourable conditions for visitors and sojourns. Everybody agrees that her tourist potentiality is immense and varied as the country offers a great choice of attractive possibilities which answer always the renewed demand of modern international travellers. The recent efforts made by the country in the field of transportation will offer the best prospects for a larger number of visitors to come and visit the country. The influx of international visitors are now on the increase. It is doing its best for the utilisation and development to the fullest extent the tourist attractions of the country, existing and potential with a view to securing maximum contribution not only to the economic development but also to the spread of international understanding and goodwill.

Tourist industry is an intra-disciplinary activity. It is made of a whole host of activities and industries, directly or indirectly affected by tourism to varying degrees. So the rapid growth of tourism and new resort development will eventually have a heavy impact on most aspects of life. Therefore, tourism implies now in our country, special care and attention at the highest level of planning in order to project long-range social and economic health of the country and pleasant environment, good ecological balance, open spaces, preservation of natural beauty, recreation facilities and convenient transport. So the need of the hour is the widespread access to tourism for all segments of the population and it scarcely constitutes factor contributing to the basic objective of raising standard of living and promoting real awareness of internal obstacles to development. It is hightime now to make facilitation measures and publicity campaigns more encouraging to provide appropriate technical and financial assistance to grant credits on easy terms and to train personnel needed for the development of tourism. It is therefore, recommended to cooperate in drawing up long term plans for the development of tourism. It is necessary to integrate tourism into national economic planning.

Y.R. Satyal

CONTENTS

1

GENERAL INFORMATION OF NEPAL

Nepal is a land of vivid colours and contrasts. It has its broad range of activities and attractions. It is regarded as one of the world's favorite vacation playground. It offers congenial climate all the year round in a spectacular setting of towering gaints of Nepal Himalaya and lush green valleys. It is, no doubt, a small country in size but it holds an unique place in the tourist map of the world with many breath-taking wonders of culture and nature. Its scenic beauty, wild animal reserves, ethnic cultures and lovely cities and villages—the place of a visit of this vast and varied country, one will find it the most rewarding of all travel experience. It covers Nature's most secret colours hidden away for ages in the singular beauty of vast mountains deep beneath variety of wonders.

Nepal, in reality, is the only country with a continent in itself but little else remains the same. Here is vacation variety unlimited. Here too, one can see and enjoy such wonders as deepest gorges, highest mountains in the world, glacier moraines, waterfalls, rocky as well as green hills, national parks and a host of other famous places and sights. It proves an opportunity for vacation paradise. The grandeur of landscape has given the country a mystical charm of its own. It is a land of vivid spectrum of beauty and colour—a panorama which is as vast as it is fascinating.

The natural landscape is majestic. Nepal Himalayas stand unchallenged, awesome and proud with their snowcapped peaks. The Himalayan ranges include most of the highest peaks of the world including Sagarmatha (Mt. Everest) the tallest peak in the world. It offers endless variety and boundless fascination of an unspoilt environment. There are so many exotic facets, natural as well as man-made arts and culture, to the arid zone in the rain shadow's of the Himalayas and cool lofty snow - capped mountains, green valleys in between animals, flowers and vegetations. It presents the opportunity to view hauntingly beautiful temples and a wealth of art and culture dating thousands of years past and to meet the hospitable people, lovely and gentle who will always wish to make the visitor feel welcome. It is a mystical typical Kaleidoscope of sensory delight. Every space gives varied visual attractions which no other country can able to provide within such a small compass.

GEOGRAPHY AND PHYSICAL FEATURES

Nepal is a land of unique attractions. The sovereign independent country situated on the southern slopes of the mid-Himalayas lies between 80°4'- 88°12'. East longitude and 26°22'- 30°27' North latitude. It is located between Tibet autonomous region of the people's Republic of China in the North and India in the South, East and West. It has an area of 14181 sq. km. The length of the country from east to west in 885 km. and its width from north to south, non-uniform is the mean width of 193 km. The major part of the country consists of high mountains and rolling hills. It accounts for about 83 percent of the total land area and the remaining 17 percent is occupied by the flat land of the Terai, an alluvial plain in the south. The altitude of the country varies from 150 meter above the sea level in the Terai in the south to more than 8,800 meter in the north Himalayas.

Nepal is known world over as the country of high mountains. It is nestled in the midst of the world's highest mountains with more than a quarter of its land over 3,000 meters in altitude. The land is rectangular in shape and roughly 40 percent of the land is cultivated and the rest is under perpetual snow, forest and river beds.

The physical feature of the country is a succession of bands passing along the east west axis. To the south is the lowland Terai, a flat tropical belt never more than 48 km (30 miles) wide. The lowland Terai region is played up by the deep and silent rivers which cascade down the mountain gorges carrying their icy waters. It is a narrow tropical area along the Indian border, compresses the northern most fringes of the Ganges plains and the first foothills of the Himalayan massif. It holds about one third of the population and two thirds of Nepal's cultivated land. It is covered by open flat countryside with tropical climate and tropical vegetation. This region shelters a wide array of wildlife including some of the last Asian rhinoceroses, elephants, wild buffaloes, tigers and deers.

From the Terai, the land rises steeply to the Mahabharat Lekh mountain ranges with peaks of up to 4,877 m. This is followed by the wide range of the Central Hills, mostly steep, rugged and an undulating mountainous area, cut through by deep valleys. The turbulent rivers pass through these mountains draining them, break out from their deep narrow gorges. Another mountain area is the Churia Hills along the southern border of Nepal. The Churia Hills, geologically a succession of the Siwalik range rise smoothly from the plains to about 1525 before becoming abrupt almost perpendicular slopes rising to an attitude of more than 3050. Within the region, there is escarpments of narrow ridges, separated by more or less wide valleys covering northwest - southwest part of it. These valleys called as "DUNS" are a dominant feature of the foothills of Nepal. Southward is situated the steeps slope known as Bhabar. South of Bhabar and the Churia Hills is the Terai—lowland of alluvial plains. This range represents as a natural wall protecting the lower middle Hills and passing north covers the actual mainland bordered by the Great Himalayan range further north.

Within the short sketch of 193 km. which separates her southern border from those of the north, Nepal soars steeply from a mere 152 m. above sea level to the towering Himalayan snowy peaks. The northern fringe is dotted with the highest peaks in the world. The Nepal Himalaya is continued in such a way to High Himalayan massifs and their famous peaks above 6000 meters to 8848 meters. They are the loftiest mountain ranges in the world and covers the world's highest and also the most majestic summits. Nepal Himalaya is not one long continuous range but of many ranges which spread in various directions. Mount Everest, the highest peak in the world (8848 m), dominates the amphitheater of Himalayan peaks and tiers of other equally dominant peaks of various hights and dimensions. From East to West Nepal the Himalayas compose of a vast cluster of mountains having more than 240 peaks of 6000 meters and above. Nepal Himalaya extends over an 800 km. with Kanchanjunga Himal in the east of Byas Rishi Himal in the west. The highest and most dramatic peaks lie to the north and in the eastern half of Nepal. These great mountain mass holds majestic splendor with spectacular Kanchanjunga, Makalu, Dhaulagiri, Annapurna, Lotse, Cho Oyu, Manaslu etc. Nepal extends beyond the Himalayan range to the Trans-Himalayan area which is part of the barren Tibetan plateau.

The great Himalayan region lies at an altitude of 4877 m to 8848 m above the sea level with the snow line running at 4877 m. The great Himalayan summits like the Kumbhakarna, the Jugal, the Mustang, the Ganesh, the Annapurna, Cho Oyu and Machhapuchhre fan out from the east to the west. The silvery peaks of Nepal Himalaya are the combination of snow, rock and ice which envelope nature's most exciting scenery. Nepal Himalaya, the highest and mightiest peaks, awesome and vast in unchallenged and isolated supremacy rise proud and majestic, mass on mass.

THE CLIMATE

Nepal has a diversity of weather and climate due to altitudinal differences. It is about 885 km (East to West) in length and 193 km (North to South) in width with altitudes varying between 152 meters in the southern Terai area bordering India to Mount Everest, a colossal 8848 meters. The country experiences tropical, sub-tropical, alpine and Trans-Himalayan types of climate.

Vegetation differs from thick jungle in the tropical forest to sub-tropical and rich pine mountain jungles ending in the north, in the wind swept arid Trans-Himalayan region. Due to altitudinal differences, the weather conditions vary from region to region. The Terai area has hot and humid climate in the summer and just cool in the winter. The average temperature rises from 21°C to 39°C in summer and 9°C to 30°C during winter. In the central mountain region, the weather is cold in the winter and just cool in the summer. The average temperature lies between 15° to 35°C in summer and 0° to 20°C during winter. The mid-land which has pockets of valleys has a warm and soothing climate. Most of the rainfall occurs during the summer season. The annual rainfall during summer varies from 60 to 100 inches while in Kathmandu valley it is about 58 inches. Pokhara valley gets more then 150 inches of rainfall during the summer.

Nepal has four seasons. The two ideal seasons are September to November and February to April, where there is little or no rain and temperature in Kathmandu are about 13°C to 24°C. The winter season, December to January, is cold about 4°C to 8°C warm clothings are necessary but it never snows. The hot season, March to August, records temperature in the range of 21°C to 35°C with the monsoon begining in mid-September. Rains are not as heavy as in other parts of Asia but humidity is high. The extreme maximum temperature 35°C in summer and extreme minimum 20°C during winter are recorded. Nepal, by virtue of its geographical setting, the climatic condition is governed by its topographical extremities. Tropical, sub-tropical, temperate, alpine, sub-alpine and tundra types of climate are respectively encountered in its Terai lowland, mid-land Hills and the alpine region. The climate of Nepal is as varied as and reflects the physical feature and altitude bands of the country. This dramatic complex and varied topography form the basis of the Tourism attractions of Nepal. It has a very pleasant climate all the year round.

FLORA AND FAUNA

Nepal, with its preeminent range of altitude (from 150 m above the sea level) in the Terai in the south to more than 8848 m in the north Himalaya, its ground preserving identity from rich alluvial places to crystalline rocks, and its rainfall from 60 to 100 inches on the outer ranges to nearly a tenth of that amount behind the great mountains, has an amaging range and variety of both flora and fauna.

The altitude variation requires a division of the country into three natural regions *i.e.* (1) Himalayan region, (2) Mountain Region and (3) Terai Region. Himalayan region and the Alpine region together have four species of willows, eight varieties of evergreen oaks, eleven rhododendrons and a dozen conifers, besides birch, alder, hornbeam, elm, poplar and the valuable walnut. Other common species include castanopises, Magnolia, Michelia, Champaca and many others. Many species of flowers as primulas, anemone, hawthorn, eglantine etc. are found.

In the Alpine Himalayan Region, dwarf rhododendron juniper and birch make way to live vigorously in resistance to snow and with increasing altitude the surviving trace of vegetation ultimately thins out to give place to barren rock and incessant ice and snow. Alpine flower "edelweiss" is found in plenty in Langtang Valley.

The variety and abundance of the fauna increase progressively with decreasing altitude and increasing growth of the vegetation. In the high alpine zone, species of animals are relatively few and include the snow leopard and marmot, ghoral, ibex and tahr, yak and the rare Tibetan stag. In this part, also are noticed some glorious pheasants, the rare blood pheasant, the beautiful tragopan and the handsome monal (IMPEYAN PHEASANT), national bird of Nepal.

The mountain region has a richer fauna. The cat species include the leopard, the superb clouded leopard and the rare golden cat, tiger, civet, Himalayan civet and paradoxurus

Jackal, wild dog and fox abound in this and the Terai region as deers, also the black Himalayan bear and ratel (badger). The gleaming sky flying squirrels, serow, the cervidae by the musk deer and the barking deer, the porcupine and mongoose, the red monkey and the grey ape (langur) are noticed in these areas. Amongst the birds of this region are the Chir and Kaliz pheasants, the chikor, black partridge and wood partridge, while various kinds of pigeon, snipe and duck are seen in the valley of Kathmandu.

The Terai region is famous by immense spread of tropical forest. The valuable shorea robusta achieves its best conditions of growth and with it are mixed many other species prominently Jamman, kadam, banyan, pipal (ficus religiosa) etc. Scantly drained areas are Savannahs of tall grasses, having optimum height of twice the size of an elephant. The river beds are covered with Dabergia Sissu and Acacia catechu respectively. The dry Churia hills yield bark grass and tall Pinus Longiflora. Orchids cover the trunks of trees and excessive overgrowth climbers cling thickly by a wide foliage.

The Terai is full of more abundant and varied fauna. The great Terai forests are the home of tiger and leopard, the sloth bear, the wild elephant, the great rhinoceros and wild buffalo, the deer species include the sambar, swamp deer, chital, hog deer and the little mouse deer, while the antelope are represented by the black buck and four horned antelope and wild pig. The principal birds of this region are the peacock, jungle fowl and black partridge while migratory duck and geese are seen on the ponds and great rivers of the Terai. The Terai region is internationally known as a haven to the lover of wild animals and bird life, to the naturalist and to the nature worshipper.

The preservation of flora and fauna in Nepal has been taken up with the creation of a chain of National Parks along with Wildlife Reserves. The National Parks and Wildlife Reserves of Nepal and divided into two categories. Firstly, Terai is represented by Royal Chitwan National Park, Koshi Tappu Wildlife Reserve, Royal Bardia National Park, Sukla phanta Wildlife Reserve etc. Secondly, Himalayan region is represented by Sagarmatha National Park, Langtang National Park, Rara National Park, Shey Phoksundo National Park, Khaptad National Park, Annapurna Conservation Area Project and Dhorpatan Hunting Reserve.

Different types of flora and fauna are preserved in Nepal's national parks and wildlife reserves scattered all over the country. The various arrangements for safari tours are organised for international visitors who are eager to view wild grandeurs in close angle with modern comforts.

THE PEOPLE

Nepal has a composite population stemming from various racial stocks. It has been a melting pot of diverse linguistic and ethnic groups. It has a population of about 20 million made of an assortment of ethnic groups, living in different regions, wearing different costumes and speaking different languages and dialects. The people belong to multi-ethnic groups, ranging from the Indo-Aryan to Mongoloid. The Himalayan and central hill regions are mostly inhabited by the people of the Tibeto-Burman strand while the people inhabiting the Terai lowlands may be grouped under the Indo-Aryan category. Its cultural traditions, art and literary heritage go back to thousands of years. The varied mosaic of various races and ethnic groups have given to Nepal a district character and culture. The Nepali language is an off-shoot of the Indo-European family of language through long association with its neighbours, it has added many Tibeto-Burman words.

In the high Himalayan region (2,438 m to 4, 877 m) live Mongoloid people. While in the northern Himalayan regions, the Sherpas, popularly known as the "Tiger of the snow". Further to the east inhabit the Bhotias, Tamangs, Limbus and Rais. In the west, mostly on the southern slopes of Annapurna mountain, Himalchuli and Ganesh Himal, the Gurungs, Magars and Sunwars live. In the heart of Nepal-Kathmandu valley live the Newars, Brahmans, Thakurs and Kshetries. The mountain region known as mid-land having 1,067 m—2,124m is inhabited by both Tibeto-Burman and Indo-Aryan people. While the Brahmins and the Kshetries are widely distributed throughout the country, Newars are assembled inside the valley of Kathmandu, in centres and outlying smaller towns.

The hill people are the Rais, the Limbus, the Tamangs the Magars, the Sunwars, the Jirels, the Gurungs, the Thakalis, the Chepangs. All of them have their own distinct social and cultural traits.

The Dun Valleys and the lowland terai are unhabited by the people among when the Brahmans, the Rajputs, the Tharus, the Danwars, the Majhis, the Derals, the Rajbansis, the Sattars, the Dhimals, the Dhangars, the Muslims add another distintive culture and racial stock. The Nepali people are divided into 45 cultural groups with mixture of casts and ethnic group.

All the people whatever their racial stock, races and tribal linkage live together peacefully to form an integral whole. They are tried up together by their common ideals of understanding and compromise. The colourful diversity of the ethnic groups is experienced only by the harmony in which the different races co-exist in one common ideal of friendliness and sense of hospitality.

CUSTOMS

Each races and tribes maintain their own tradition, culture, social life, moral values, dress, habits and way of life. So the customs of the people are different in various places. In the midst of this apparent multiplicity of religious faiths and ritual practices, the most significant fact is that in actual everyday life the sects and denominations merge into one another to form one unified nationality. All Gods and Goddesses command the deep respect of all. Similarly, the festivals connected with this or that deity is happily shared by all, synthesis not atheism, popularisation, not polarisation, heterodoxy not orthodoxy, is the main spring of Nepali way of life. Nepal from time immemorial has most handsomely maintained a very singular tradition of religious tolerence and amicable co-existence among different faiths.

RELIGION

Hinduism and Buddhism constitute two major religions of the country. Nepal is a country with a multiracial and multilingual community. Hindus and Buddhists co-exist together to comprise one concordant social system. Nepal's population is constituted of 89.5 percent Hindus and 5.3 percent Buddhists but Hinduism and Buddhism are both equally honoured in Nepal and the blending of the two religions into one entity have inspired and created the distant culture of its order. The reflection of these uniqueness of Nepali culture can be seen in the every day life of people and in the works of arts and architectures. There are many castes and creeds but no rigidity. There is religious tolerance everywhere. All the God and Goddesses are worshipped by the Hindus as well as the Buddhists according to their religious rites. The Kumari, or Vestil virgin Goddess of Kathmandu, for instance is a Hindu Goddess but selected from a Buddhist clan for worship. It is not unusual to have a Hindu temple within Buddhist establishments and *vice versa*.

Nepal is the birth place of Sita, the consort of Lord Rama, who is the hero of the Hindu epic Ramayana. It is also the birth place of Sakyamuni Gautama Buddha who gave the world a message of philosophy of peace, tolerance and compassion. Nepal is full of Hindu and Buddhist shrines, monuments, temples, and stupas of these Gods. Through the courses of history, both Hinduism and Buddhism provided inspiration to Nepali folklore, art, architecture, music, dance, and festivals combining to form unique and charming religious tradition for all the people of Nepal.

ART AND CULTURE

Nepal is not only a country of geomorphological attraction but also an anthropological odd. These are various ethnic groups in Nepal co-exist and this character has created an unique and distinct culture in Asia. They have constructed temple, stupas images and offered ceremonies and festivals to deities of both Hinduism and Buddhist in one of the eyes of these deities by preserving their cultural heritage and religious traditions. Its culture dates back thousand of years and the country is a varitable museum of artistic treasures, magnificent shrines and temples and other lavishly decorated edifices, images and carvings of exquisite design all competing with scenic mountain grandeur unequaled anywhere, exotic flora and the richest sanctuary of wildlife. The character of Nepali culture is unity in diversity. Nepali culture is a mixture of two different civilizations of Asia-Mongoloid and Indo-Aryan culture. The ethnic stock and their customs are different in various parts of the country. But the people form one entity and represents a picture not only of a different features but living peacefully in co-existence in an amicable and harmonious atmosphere.

Hinduism and Buddhism are both equally honoured in Nepal and the blending of the two religions into one entity have inspired and created a distinct culture of its own. Though it is too small country, nearly 147,181 sq. km. but it maintained the scene of a cultural prosperity remarkable even in the eyes of the Nepal's neighbours, India and Tibet. It had not copied the all influences of the civilization of the two neighbours but developed indigenous elements of their own for creating heterogenous ethnic and cultural characteristics into a distinctive pattern. It is a plain fact that the kingdom of Nepal since time immemorial has exerted a remarkable influence on the neighbouring countries while maintaining an independent existance. The Kathmandu valley has enjoyed continuous development even if it has the effect of exodous of immigrants. The Kathmandu valley, a cultural seat of Nepal has survived the priceless testimonies of Nepali culture presenting both the high ideal and ingenuity of its own.

The arts and tradition of Nepal, inspired by ancient Hindu and Buddhist cultures are of an astonishing richness specially in the valley of Kathmandu. Many buildings testify Pagoda style of architecture and numerous predominent temples and shrines of the early Lichhavi and Malla periods stand in cities and are scattered throughout countryside and are even in villages. The architectural and artistic standard of these periods not only document the excellent masterpieces in the part of Asia (12th Century AD) but is a priceless cultural contribution to the history of mankind.

Relics of the ancient period and of the following architectural trends of the 16th century are also present among the masterpieces found in Nepal. All these architectural buildings are accompanied by combines and series of artistic works—paintings, sculptures from each respective period of history and are supplemented by objects of daily uses. Often palaces and temples house the complete equipment of artisan workshops and other production means of various begone ages. Bhaktapur Art Gallery collections acquaint visitors with the wide range of masterpieces of paintings. These are also original collections of period—clothing both civil, religious and theatrical costumes which can be seen in festival and other special occassions. All these historical artifacts represent an immense wealth of national tradition and culture.

The Nepalese year is an unending cycle of festivals. Hindu Gods and Buddhist deities are placed side by side. The people pay divine honours to both with the same reverence. The festivals in general, one connected with the episodes or admiration from the famous Hindu scripture or Buddhist mythology. All these festivals are celebrated somehow or other according to age-old tradition. Picturesque pageantry ceremonials both gay and solemn and the ardent ferver of a nation are elegantly displayed during the important national festivals of Nepal. These conspicuous events are the heritage of an ancient culture.

Nepal is the meeting ground of the great civilizations of Asia and as such it is the cultural museum where art treasures and monuments of historical interest are preserved. The annals of the Chinese Tang dynasty contain several references to the people of Nepal and its art and living around the middle of the 7th century A.D. The spread of Tantric Vajrayana from the 7th-8th century onwards from Nepal to Tibet where it developed into Lamaism exerted an influence upon the

Mongols from the 13th, and especially from the 16th century. Tibetan art developed out of Nepali and Chinese elements.

Chinese envoys who visited Nepal in Lichhavi era has given accounts of the rich prosperity and the high standard of art and architecture. By the description of the Chinese enjoy, it is proved that the Pagoda style was firstly evolved and developed in Nepal as he had not seen such architecture before. This style of architecture spread from Nepal to many other Asian countries in succession of times.

Nepali people from ancient time, are freedom loving people, therefore they have never been subjected to external dominance or colony. The high snowy mountains have been helpful in the development of the ideas of freedom, adventure and romance. Vagaries of different climate with variation in altitudes have effected the temper and needs of the Nepali people. The people differ not only in the physical appearances but also in moral traits. The first traits of general character in their outward reserve—frigidity and stuborness. They are warm-hearted and hospitable. In reality, Nepali people is hard-headed. In each and every Nepali people, there is a sense of order—not imposed from without but grows from within. It is perhaps a heritage of centuries of freedom. They are proud of their tradition.

Nepali people have a flexible temperament. There is no doubt, caste system in Nepal. There are many castes and creeds but no regidity. There is religious tolerance everywhere. Everything is based on compromise and understanding. The Nepali people and their way of life act as a major attraction to international visitors and represent an important facet to cultural tourism. The Nepali warmth and friendliness towards visitor is part of their lofty magnitude of tolerance towards alian culture and religións evolved through a long history of close contact with the people of neighbouring countries. Economically, the people of Nepal is not so rich but they are happy breed of men, proud of their glorious past and sure of the valuable future that lies ahead of them. Due to their long tradition and glorious history, they are free from all kinds of inner stress. They have, therefore, the broadest grin in the whole of Asia.

Nepal has maintained religion such as Hinduism, Buddhism, and Shaivism and Vaishnavism and practices throughout the years. Buddhism is closely associated to Hinduism. It has influenced deep into the Nepali life. I the second half of the first millennium, Nepal came under the influence of religious movement that incorporated ideas of sinister spiritual power, magic forces, necromancy and a great variety of symbols. The first period coming to the end of the 12th century A.D. was marked by a fervent religious activity of a Tantric variety, a left hand cult with its elevation of the female or Sakti element and sex were freely introduced in both Shaivism and Buddhism. The unifying force in this seeming diversity is Tantricism. It unites Sakti, Shiva and Vaishnava and known as Bajrayana a Buddhist terminology and its influence is pervaded all the religious practices relating to various sects. Some sects also workship nature or shamanism. Very few Nepali follow to Islam and Christianity. The well-set principle of acceptance and assimilation has been the all embracing mainspring for the integrity of Nepal culture.

Nepal has a history spreading thousands of years. Its advancement in art and architectural beauties, organised social, religious economic and political system developed by the people through centuries and harmonious livings by them whatever their racial stocks and creeds and a common language, Nepali have contributed the unique Nepali culture preserved and cherished by all.

The age-old cultural heritage of Nepal has inspired the growth of a splendid art and architectural tradition. The arts and crafts of Nepal, fostered by ancient Hindu and Buddhist culture, are of an astonishing richness, especially in the valley of Kathmandu.

Nepal is the cultural museum where art treasures and monuments of historical interest are presented. Kathmandu, with Patan and Bhadgaon, second and third towns in importance constitute a rare ensemble of an architecture of great originality and quality. Innumerable temples both pagoda and stupas and thousands of interesting other monuments and private houses with carved doors, balconies and windows testify to the rich cultural tradition which inspired the people to create and embellish them. The range of architecture in Nepal is varried and unlimited as so with the sculpture and they are demonstrated from the diagrams or pictures, temples and stupas to the abstraction of the Mandala. The architecture of Nepal is simple and plain but decorative, pleasently striking in grace and appearance.

Nepal is a most colourful country with a charm blend of Asian cultures. An abundance of temples, stupas, monasteries and Durbar complex of tri-cities of Kathmandu valley makes the country a land of devotees who keep alive a deep religious heritage. So far as the arts and architecture are concerned, Nepal is a loveliar place than this the heart of man could scanty desire. The prevalance of craftsmanship reflects the works of many craftsman continuing their arts over the centuries.

The exquisite architecture and artistic embellishment of Nepali Pagodas that enshrine the bronze, stone images and structs of temples, windows and doors with carved wooden figures of great beauty and more often than not, great antiquity are a unique feature of Nepal.

The temples, stupas, monasteries and Gompas are rich repository of wood carving, metal working, terracotta and stone sculpture. In their uniqueness, they add gory and grandeur to the cultural scene of the country and tell of a long history of nature genius. Down the centuries, both Hinduism and Buddhism have provided inspiration to Nepali folklore and art, combining to form unique and charming religious tradition for all Nepali.

The civilisation of Nepal goes back thousand of years before the birth of Christ. The arts of the Nepali people stem from a cultural tradition which has produced a rich array of bewitching creation in every form of art.

HISTORY

With a civilization stretching back to thousands of years, Nepal, no doubt, has lent magnificence due to its unforgetable scene, historical places, traditional artistry and the rich cultural heritage. The early history of Nepal is not readily available and is shrouded in legends and mythology. One such legend tells the story of Manjushri Praddhi Satava who cut an opening at the rockhill at chover by his magical scimitar and drained the lake water to make the Kathmandu valley good for human settlement. In another mythological account, a hermit known as "Ne" was the first to populate and protect Nepal and so Nepal means a land created and protected by the saint Ne.

The Nepali genealogy mention without any corroborative evidence that the first ruling dynasty were Gopalas, the Abhirs and the Kiratees in early days. King Dharmakar was the first king in the Gopala dynasty.

After the decline of Gopala Dynasty, the Kirata dynasty came to power, Yalamber was the first king in the dynasty. Recorded history begins with the Lichhavis after the fall of Kirata and other dynasties. The authentic history begins with the Changu Narayan Pillar Inscription of Licchavic King Mana Devi of the 5th century. The Lichhavis ruled over Nepal from 5th Century A.D. and the country achieved a high degree of progress in art and architecture, industry, commerce and religious beliefs and foreign relations.

Another important Lichhavi monarch was Amshu Verma who opened trade routes to Tibet and one of his daughters, Bhrikuti, who was given in Marriage to Tibetan ruler Tsrong-Tsang Compo was instrumented in spreading the Gospel of the Buddha in Tibet and China. The princess converted the king to Buddhism and she is revered as the founder of Tibet Buddhism.

Narendra Deva, another Lichhavic king initiated friendly relations with China and his successors laid the foundation of friendships with India by entering into matrimonial alliance with the Indian royal families.

Accounts of a Chinese envoy who visited the valley during Narendra Deva's rule testify to the economic prosperity and well being of the country. The palace of Narendra Deva described in detail by the Chinese envoy provides proof of the fact that pagoda style of architecture was evolved and developed in Nepal. It spread from Nepal to many eastern countries in subsequent centuries.

From the 13th to the 18th century, the Malla Dynasty took over the leadership of the country and became the king of Kathmandu as well as of the other surrounding areas. The Malla Dynasty's rule set the medieval history of Nepal. Soon afterwards at the end of the fifteenth century the Kingdom of Nepal was divided into three kingdoms by the sons of King Yakshya Malla of Kathmandu Valley. The United Kingdom was divided into tree independent principalities namely Kathmandu, Patan and Bhadgaon. The kings of these kingdoms were constantly involved in disputes and wars. They were weakened because of constant wars. Inspite of debilitating wars, the kings of these principalities vied with each other to decorate their capitals with artistic and beautiful palaces, temples and other masterpieces of buildings which are considered to be the pride of Nepal at the present time. Besides, the kings of these states were great patrons and lovers of art, architecture and introduced various religious ceremonies and dances.

Pratap Malla (1640-1763) and more so Bhupatendra Mala (1696-1722) of Kathmandu and Bhadgaon were among those who not only increased their territory and the political importance of their respective kingdoms but also decorated their main capitals with many temples, pagodas, palaces, fountain and public baths. They also promoted the development of handicraft in wood, stone, ivory, gold and silver.

At the start of the modern period, Nepal divided into inmemorable principalities—Kathmandu valley into varies states. There were Baisi (22 small independent states) and Chaubisi (24 principalities). It was the Gorkha King, Prithivi

Narayan Shah the great (A.D. 1722-1774), who united all the small and divergent warring states into a United Nepal. King Prithivi Narayan Shah, was born in 1722 and ascended the throne of Gorkha in 1743. His dreams and the ambitions were to unify the whole of the country. It took him almost 25 years of almost uninterrupted wars and diplomacy. Ultimately be succeeded in 1774 and united all the small and divergent warning principalities into a United Nepal. King Prithivi Narayan Shah succeeded by his eldest son and after that his grandson Rana Bahadur Shah. The Nepali had differences with East India Company regards the ownership of the land of the western Terai. The rulers had to face the mighty British expansion in the Asian sub-continent which terminated in a British-Gorkha war with the British East India Company. The war ended in a compromise settlement which fixed the frontier of Nepal territories still are to day. Following this, there was a power struggle among the nobles of the court during the reign of the King Rajendra Bikram Shah. Jung Bahadur Rana came into power by bloody massacre of his opponent nobles in Kot Massacre in 1846. The Ranas ruled from 1846 to 1950. Thus Rana family weilded all political power and imposed family autocratic rule in Nepal. They served only their personal interests trying to keep the King and the people in utter darkness. During 104 years of the Rana oligarchy, Nepal remained a closed country.

The autocratic Rana regime came to an end in November 1950, when King Tribhuvan led a popular revolt against the Rana autocracy. On February 15, 1951, King Tribhuvan laid the foundation of non-autocratic regime.

King Tribhuvan died in 1955 and his eldest son Mahendra Bir Bickram Shah Dev succeeded to the throne. A parliamentary form of government was set up. Nepal became the member of the United Nations in 1955 and also became the member of the Security council of the world body in 1969 and 1970. Nepal also extended diplomatic relations with many countries. But the King Mahendra took the royal take over in 1960 and launched partyless Panchayat system.

Present King, His Majesty King Birendra Bir Bickram Shah Dev succeeded the throne on January 31, 1972 upon the demise of the late king Mahendra Bir Bickram Shah Dev. His Majesty Birendra Bir Bickram Shah Dev played an active role in establishing South Asian Association for Regional Cooperation at the Dhaka Summit in 7-8 December 1989 in Bangladesh. The movement for the establishment of democracy started by the people in 1990 as against the Partyless Panchayat system. The people movement of 1990 reinstated the multi-party democratic system. The new democratic constitution of Nepal was drafted and promulgated on November 9, 1990. Now, Nepal is marching ahead with multi-party democratic system and is engaged for making all round development of the country. Democracy has emerged as the only viable political system following the restoration of democracy and multi-party system in Nepal. But the structure of democracy however in very fragile in Nepal to-day. The democratic evolution is to be practiced and perfected by all concerned to make it successful and workable.

2

TOURISM IN NEPAL

Tourism is a recent phenomenon to Nepal. Nepal opened the doors to international visitors only towards the end of 1950. The promotion of tourism in the true sense started more or less only from the beginning of the 1960's. Nepal became the member of International Union of Official Travel Organisation (IUOTO) in 1959 (New World Tourism Organisation) and Pacific Area Travel Association in 1964. Since then, Nepal took part in the International Tourism Conferences, seminars, fairs and exhibitions to expose the image of Nepal to the international tourists.

A Tourist Development Board was set up by His Majesty's Government of Nepal in November 1957 and the Board was replaced by the full-fledged Department of Tourism within the Ministry of Public Works, Transport and Communication in 1962. It was in 1967 that the Department of Tourism was transferred to the wing of Ministry of Commerce and industry. The Department of Tourism functioned under various ministries up to the end of February 23, 1977, when a separate Ministry of Tourism was formed to look after tourism development.

Since its establishment, the Department of Tourism has made surprising headway as is evidence by the creation of tourist countries, regulating the hotel, lodges and other catering industries, issuance of the recommendation of licences for the running and establishment of hotel industries, activities with a view to the abolition, relaxation and simplification of entry and departure formalities of foreign visitors, and encouraging adhesion of international conventions in favour of tourism and the application of their provisions.

The Ministry of Tourism and Civil Aviation now functions as the National Tourism Organisation and is responsible for all policy matters relating to tourism of the national and international level. The Department of Tourism was the main organ for the execution of the policy set down by the Ministry of Tourism. The broad objective of the Tourist Department was to stimulate tourist travel to Nepal. This involved publicity concerning the attraction of Nepal to interested persons, the improvement of hotels and making other facilities available to tourists to ensure a favourable reaction by visitors to this country.

The Department of Tourism established tourist information centres at Different places like Pokhara, Bhairawa, Birgunj, Kakarvita, Jomsom Janakpur, Pashupatinath, Tribhuvan Airport and in the city centre of Basantpur, Kathmandu. The Tourist Bunglow at Nagarkot, Kakani, Daman and Pokhara firstly established by the Department of Tourism to cater for international visitors, have been given now to Tara Gaon Development Board in pursuit of the policy of His Majesty's Government to encourage the private sector in the accommodation business.

Ministry of Tourism and Civil Aviation and the Department of Tourism play and important part in the promotion of tourism abroad. His Majesty's Government Department of Tourism promoted itself by distributing of tourist literature by direct mail, participating in fairs and exhibitions, advertising in travel trade journals and by association with international conferences. It also cooperated with diplomatic and consular representatives abroad for distribution of publicity materials and the supply of tourist information. Along with the coming of Tourism Council and Tourism Board, now a major change in His Majesty's Government Department directly related to tourism occured as for example Department of Tourism abolished and the Department of Civil Aviation became an autonomous body—

Nepal Civil Aviation Authority since December 1998. The Nepal Tourism Board is just initiated and it should now immediately start work efficiently all the activities within its scope, proving worthy of its creation.

In order to provide a planned development of tourism, His Majesty's Government secured the services of a consulting team in cooperation with the Government of the Federal Republic of Germany. The project was assigned to a group of experts in March 1971 by the Federal Agency for development aid in its capacity as executing agency for the Federal Ministry of Economic Cooperation. A preliminary action programme was prepared and submitted to His Majesty's Government of Nepal in August 1971. The Master Plan for Tourism was prepared and submitted in its final shape in 1972 and was approved by His Majesty Government in August 1972. The concrete steps to promote and develop tourism were made when a high level "Nepal Tourism Development Committee" was constituted in 1971 and the Nepal Tourism Master Plan prepared in 1972.

Tourism development and its importance have recently be realized in Nepal. Its importance as social and economic force had not been received the impetus as it is receiving today. First Five Year Plan (1956-1961) was formed which enclosed provision for tourism for the first time in the history of Nepal. After the First Five Year Plan successive Five Year Plans *i.e.* the Second Five Year Plan (1962-65), Third Plan 1965-66—1969-70, Fourth Five Year Plan (1970-75), Fifth Five Year Plan (1975-80), Sixth Five Year Plan (1980-1985), Seventh Five Year Plan (1985-90) and the Eighth Plan (1992-1997), now Ninth Five Year Plan on the move and all these plans place emphasis on the development of tourism for the creation of employment and augmentation of foreign exchange.

Tourism in Nepal has increased dramatically in recent years. Nepal received 6179 international visitors in 1962 but by the end of 1990, this figure reached 254,885 tourist arrivals. Tourist arrival reached the figures of 326,531 in 1994 more than 11.2 percent as compared to 1993 by the tourist arrivals of

293,567. Then in 1995, there were 363,395, a change of 8.3 percent of Tourist arrivals as compared with the figures of 393,613 tourist arrivals in 1996. The average length of stay of tourists in 1993 was about 12 days which has not changed much since 1974 when it was 13 days. Foreign exchange earning from tourism has been increasing. The foreign exchange earning from Tourism in 1993-94 was Rs. 8251.7 million where as it increased by 8.7 percent to Rs. 8973.2 million in 1994-95. The earning in 1996 reached to the figure of 6599700. Another important advantage of tourism is labour intensive and has been able to provide gainful employment generation in various fields.

Figures revel that the number of tourist arrivals is increasing every year. In 1997 Nepal received 396 thousand tourist and it is expected that visit Nepal Year 1998 will succeed in the targeted figure of five hundred thousand tourists. But visit Nepal now come to a close but the figures of tourists are not able to attract the targeted tourists. In such a way, the annual growth of tourist arrivals counted about 8 percent over last 20 years. The length of tourist stay in Nepal consists from 10 to 13 days. This is all to the cause of the tourist movement is upto the present limited to some parts of the country due to lack of new destinations.

In order to meet the demands of tourist, Nepal has increased the accommodation facilities Nepal is undergoing a viritable base in accommodation. A couple of years ago, there were only about 1000 officially classified hotel rooms in the whole country and that means in particular a shortage in the more deluxe categories. In 1995, the number of hotels (star as well as non-star) and the number of hotel rooms 520 and 21,807 beds respectively. Likewise, the number of hotels reached 632 in 1996 with the capacity of 13084 rooms and 25638 beds for the tourists. The highest rate of employment is in the hotel business. Hotels now can accommodate number of tourists at a time.

The tourist centres presently in operation are the outskirts of Kathmandu, Pokhara in the West Nepal, Chitwan on the south, Sangboehe, Langtang Helambu and Manag in the north and pilgrimage centres at Janakpur and Lumbini in the south.

These have been a programme prepared with the technical assistance of Pacific Area Travel Association to develop Pokhara as a secondary tourist destination. Tourist facilities of Pokhara are improved and the Tourist Information Centre is upgrated to man and manage the tourism activities effectively.

Many tourist places or potential tourist areas are surveyed and steps are taken for their development, construction of infrastructures such as hotel, lodges and other receptive services.

More emphasis laid on improving various facilities in areas where visitor can enjoy trekking in an unspoilt natural setting. Nepal is known as the land of Himalayas, its green valleys and hospitable people. In recognizing the visitor's aptitudes for viewing awesome Nepal Himalaya and their majestic scenery, policy and programme is stressing more and more upon the development of Mountain Tourism. The number of mountaineering expeditions coming every year, the increasing number of scientific exploration teams to study the fauna, flora, geology and zoology and the increasing number of the trekkers going into the interior of Nepal bear testimony to this fact.

Trekking is immensely popular among tourists who visit the country. From about 4000 trekkers in 1971, the number reached 76856 in 1994. New trekking areas are just opened in many part of the country and 18 smaller peaks have been designated as trekking peaks. Regions such as Jomsom, Manang, Lomanting, Dolpo, Mustang etc. are among the new additions to the already famous Everest region, Rolwaling, Langtang, Gosainkunda, Mustang, Jumla and many others. The maintenance of terrain, bridges, resting lodges and drinking facilities in all areas are getting due priority. Now 342 trekking agencies are offering services to the international visitors.

As regards the protection of tourist resources, Nepal is resolved to cope with the current tendency to destroy nature and pollute the environment in the country and to preserve and utilize nature as the foundation of a wild-oriented tourism activity. Recognizing the importance of nature and natural resources of the country, His Majesty's Government of Nepal approved a comprehensive conservation scheme in 1973. The National Parks and wildlife reserves have been into establishment. There are now many national parks and wildlife reserves in the country.

As tourism is a fast growing industry more promotional efforts have to be made so that many international visitors acquaint with the charm and facilities which Nepal has to offer them in order to focus Nepal in the international Arena. His Majesty's Government, Ministry of Tourism and Civil Aviation Department of Tourism, in collaboration with all the segments of travel trade has initiated plans and programmes to take part jointly in international tourism conferences, fairs, exhibition and seminars. Many information booklets, brochures, posters, stickers etc. are published for distribution.

For the fulfilment of the requirement of manpower needed for the growing travel trade industry, His Majesty's Government established in 1972, a Vocational Institute known as the Hotel Management and Tourism Training Centre with the Assistance of UNDP/ILO. The Centre started its activities of instruction since 1973. The Centre has now plans on the way for providing high level training facilities for a larger output than at present. Many private training centres for tourism are also opened to train and manage technical manpower need of Tourism.

Despite impressive earning and growing number of visitors coming every year, tourism remains one of Nepal most unexploited resources. The unique natural and man-made attractions which the country offers, it becames obvious that, with continued proper development, tourism related activities, will form a major segment of the key industry of the country, producing a large share of the national income.

In order to get maximum benefit out of tourism and reduce its negative aspects to the minimum, His Majesty's Government is doing its best to make planned development of tourism, to market and to implement it within the framework of Nepalese prospectives. As such, tourism and its growth should be put into its amicable prospectives as far as its development goal goes with national economy and national culture.

His Majesty's Government's policy is reasonably liberal and congenial towards encouraging all the private enterprises directly or indirectly associated with the travel trade. It encourages to come up actively in establishing various tourism service industries. In this context, it may be well worthwhile to point out that the policy of His Majesty's Government has so far been to give free hand to the private enterprises in the setting up of hotel and offer service industries with tax holidays and other incentives admissible under the Nepal Industrial Enterprises Act 1962 and the Industrial Policy and Acts of Nepal (amendments) 1981 and 1987. Industries have been classified and tourism is included as one of the industries in this act. Enterprises such as tourist lodges, motels, hotels, resort areas, trekking and travel agencies, sking, water-rafting, cable car complex, trekking, hot air balloning and para-sailing which directly help, support or assist in the promotion of tourism are classified as tourism industries. Loans are also made available to them through financial organization like the Nepal Industrial Development Corporation and banks. The magnificent response which the private capital has given to this liberal policy is worth the lofty respect. Pitted against the irksomeness of the early fifties what we have now by way of variety of accommodation facilities stands at the degree of affluence. So far as the low costing lodging houses are concerned, they are in the midst of plenty. The hotels in the higher grades are also going through energetic activity to meet the demands of affluent tourists.

Measures for the simplification of the existing formalities developing upgrading accommodation and transport facilities and creating new areas are going on simultaneously. The frontier formalities are simplified. The Tribhuwan International Airport being the only airport for international entry into Nepal has an outstanding role to fulfil in the tourism development. To fulfill the requirement necessary for the international visitors, the construction of International Terminal building, airlines offices, airport operation and Central Tower was completed now. The runway of the Tribhuwan International Airport is now expanded and bigger aircrafts like the boing 707 type can take-off and land. Navigational equipments are also improved and expanded for making night landing easy and possible. Airlines of different nations for services in Nepal have increased their flight capacity and frequency. The development of air transport is taking place in Nepal with an improvement of ground and terminal facilities in the existing airports including installation of stop facilities as well as the modernization of the flying equipments owned by the national flag carrier—Royal Nepal Airlines Corporation. Royal Nepal Airlines Corporation came into existence in 1st July 1958 with mixed government and private capital. The Department of Civil Aviation was formerly created under the Ministry of Public Works and Transport in 1965. The Department of Civil Aviation/Royal Nepal Airlines became the wing of the Ministry of Tourism in 1982. Top most priority has been assigned to the development of air transport as a vehicles of accomplishing facilities of transport and communication to the remote and mountaineous parts of the country and the promotion of tourist industry. There are 43 domestic airports and stol fields of different category in the country. Within a very short span of time, the fleet modernization and up-gradation activity of the airline has enabled it to extend flight to different parts of the world which imparts a greater significance in tourism perspective of the country. There are helicopter companies and provide services on charter basis.

The number of foreign carrier's operation in Nepal has now not only increased in number but their flight frequency has also increased significantly. Non-scheduled international flights have also been started operation and with this kind of operation by a charter line started from 1971. Charter Tourism has introduced a new era of tourism in Nepal. It has given a decisive impact on international tourism by the increasing figures of international tourist flow to Nepal, His Majesty's Government of Nepal has now given permission for private sector to operate domestic airlines. These private airlines are operating scheduled flights to different parts of the country along with mountain flights daily.

In order to fulfill the need of surface transportation, the massive road building activity as now underway in different parts of the country. Nepal is now easily accessible by land route as well. Since last two decades, much has been done to improve transportation infrastructures. The recent efforts made by the country in the field of transportation with many highways with link in India on the south and with Tibet, autonomous region of the Peoples Republic of China and many feeder roads have helped open up the interior of Nepal to international tourists.

A larger choice of products is now offered to international visitors and the Travel, trekking, rafting and wildlife safari agents in Nepal have improved their receptive services, their equipments and the quality of personnel. There has been an increase in the operation of travel and trekking agencies. There were hardly 3 to 4 travel agencies to the early sixties and even by 1970 less than a dozen travel and trekking agencies were functioning. They have now increased by large numbers. This increase tends to reflect not only the increased volume of visits or influx of the international visitors but also the positive hopes of private sector enterprises for business opportunities. The summary of tourism statistics 1996 shows that there are total number of registered trekking agencies 342 and Travel Agencies—425 in numbers.

His Majesty's Government of Nepal has realized mountaineering as a valuable assets for the development of tourism. The Nepal Himalayas constitute one of the remarkable features of the Nepali landscape. It is the loftiest mountain ranges in the world and include the world's highest peaks. They stand as the dominant part of the great arch of the Himalayas. From East to West Nepal, the Himalayas compose of an exceedingly greatest mass of mountains having more then

7600 meters, topped by 8848 meters Mount Everest, the highest peak in the world together with some ten peaks of our 8000 meters and about two hundred 4877 meters peaks. The Himalayan chains like the Kumbhakarna, the Jugal and the Machhapuchhre fan out from the east to the west. In this region, the world's famous peaks of Mount Everest (8848 ι), Kanchanjunga (8585 m), Makalu (850 m), Dhaulagiri (8167 m) and Annapurna (8091 m) are located. Due to these row of mountain peaks of different sizes and dimensions, Nepal Himalayas are of exceptional attractions for the mountaineers. There is nothing to excel or complete the severity of these lofty peaks and episodic drama of their glaciers. The first endeavour to climb Sagarmatha (Mount Everest), the highest peak in the world, was made as early as 1922 A.D. but since 1949, as far as mountaineering is concerned can be called the first decade of expedition. The Nepal Himalayas have since become a great centre of mountaineering activities. Nepal offers one of the unique itineraries for the alpinets all the world over as a part of adventure tourism. The Nepal Himalayas has thus encased and attested many achievements and tragedies in the last decade.

Mountaineering has been attracting a large number of mountaineers from all over the world. It has been playing an increasingly important role in employment over the years. In FY 1993/94, altogether 105 expedition teams got permit for mountaineering with direct employment to 239 persons and royalties amounting to Rs. 44498 million. However in FY 1994/95 permit for mountaineering was granted to 91 expeditions teams for which 5795 persons got employment and accured royalties Rs. 37,307 million.

TOURISM PROSPECTS

International Tourism is almost a natural resource of Nepal. On top of natural attractions of Nepal rest the majestic Himalayas including the highest peak in the world Mount Everest and the verdant valleys under the shadow of many other peaks and remarkable geological formations. Similarly, the unique culture of Nepal has proved a constant source of information for the foreign visitors of all ages. Hinduism and Buddhism are both equally honoured in Nepal and the blending of the two religions in one entity have inspired and developed the distinct culture of its own. The picture of these uniqueness of Nepali culture can be seen in the everyday life of the people and in the works of arts and architectures which are so abundant in Nepal. Folklore, music and dances can be appreciated everywhere in the country and all the year round religious festivals bring life and colour around all temple and stupas.

Nepal's tourism image at present is leaned on adventure holiday in the Himalayas, of culture in the Kathmandu Valley and warm Nepali Hospitality. The image is of lasting nature which other countries can not rival in anyway. Nepal, therefore has developed tourism within this image with the purpose of increasing numbers and their length of stay in Nepal as a destination. Various areas of Nepal have been promoted with diverging emphasis with the overall image depending on their particular resources. While promoting tourism along there lines, the product should be:

Nature Cultural Endowment

Nepal is popular all over the world as natural playground. The combination of artistic creations of man and varied natural attractions, the instransient products of man and nature lends to Nepal a charm and individuality which is exceptional and distinct. Profuse gifts of nature in flora as well as fauna have invested Nepal with that three dimensional appeal which is so envigorating. Many architectural wonders executed with a daring richness of detail and a delicate touch which are fully traditional to charm with stupendous wonder. The colossal Himalayan summits epitomize the embattled rampart of many a mountaineering expedition and a high hope of search and adventure. The eerie depth of the deepest gorge in the world cut by tectonic snow-fed rivers flowing through the bank of ageless enchantment of the picturesque valleys, all create a fantasy of unbelievable realm that is destination Nepal.

Sunshine and azure sky is the mood of the outdoor scenes

of Nepal. An impression of innovation and sublime simplicity is created by the landscape which is interblend with the plain living of people. To be precise, Nepal is one of those few countries of the world which has got something for everybody leisure and repose.

Considering ample resources in Nepal these can be induced to achieve maximum developments on tourism substantiating through the channel of its as revenues, jobs and a better quality of life. The main basis for Nepal Tourism potential are very large area of unspoiled countryside of exceptional variety and beauty. Side by side with it, Nepal is also a melting pot of many races and tribes. All these people co-exist peacefully and pass a happy life. While having mosaic of races and tribes a remarkability express national identity through national language, national dress, music, dance customs and architecture. For these reasons, Nepal is regarded as a destination that will be visited for its own sake. Nepal is known for its pleasant climate all the year round. The Nepali people and their way of life act as a major attraction to visitors and represent an important facet to cultural tourism. Due to these spectacular attractions, there has been an exceptional growth of tourism for the past 20 years. With the expanding air and land transportation and the increase in accommodation services have been helping much for the development of tourism in the country inspite of the recumbent political and natural crisis curbed in some years badly. Many people find opportunity in various kinds of jobs related with tourism industries.

As a result of two decades of progress in tourism, it is crystal clear that the tourist target aimed at, can not attain as envisaged, taking into account the lessons of the past and the current changes accuring the world and in the industry and services connected with tourism. These aims will be worked out by explaining future relation between major tourist generating countries and new emerging countries of South Asia and Far East, so that the economics of the country may benefit from foreign exchange earnings and the creation of more jobs.

Efforts will also be made to expand travel demand and improve environment conditions, preventing political disturbances while everything must be done to promote the beneficial effects of tourism. What matters most of all is to prevent the happening of past errors and practices harmful to its social nature? Notwithstanding the many political and natural hazards which have affected the tourism industries in the country during the last few years travel and tourism continue to grow on the country at a very healthy and dramatic pace. On the other hand, however the emergence of democratic system of government in the country have produced issues and developed situations which harbour to adjust sound development of tourism in the years to come in the country.

The setting up to His Majesty's Government of Nepal, organisation for the development of tourism (in 1950) helped much for promoting the development of tourism, giving of licence for the establishment of hotels and other amenities generally to encourage and provide for taking of holidays in Nepal. Since then the role of tourism within the economy has been clearly identified and more refined objectives have now been drawn up by Tourism Policy - 1995. This New Tourism policy was approved by His Majesty's Government of Nepal which was adopted along with suggestions by the June 14, 1995. Third Tourism Council meeting held under the chairmanship of Prime Minister and the Tourism Council Chairman and was approved by the Cabinet on June 22, 1995. With the publication and enforcement of Tourism Policy 1995, both the public and private sectors in Tourism are confident of the balanced and dynamic development of tourism sector in the coming days. The Tourism Policy has precisely provided for a 30 member Tourism Council to be formed under the chairmanship of the Prime Minister. At the same Tourism Policy it is noted that His Majesty's Government of Nepal will nominate 8 to 10 persons from among sectors concerned and private experts to Tourism Development Board, appointing member-secretary of it from among its members. This Tourism Policy 1995 has also classified tourism industries. As regards the facilities and allowances to be sanctioned for the tourism and its related industries, a 10 - members Nepal Tourism Board with Government officials and representations from the private sector of the tourism services should contribute to the development of tourism in an integrated manner concerted efforts of the governmental and non-governmental agencies stand in progress or get the better of advancing as the tourism industry would be more organised. There is lack of tourism promotion and development of the tourism infrastructures in the tourist destinations all over the country. The Board has been vested with the responsibility of guiding and taking the right way for the tourism sector in Nepal.

The Tourism Board is also constituted now. The constitution of a ten member Nepal Tourism Board with government officials and representatives from the private sector as members related in the Tourism sector should contribute for the development of tourism now.

By resolutely following on the bases of past experience, a search of the true nature of tourism and by determining the new responsibilities of those who engage in this sector will mark and to catalyse all necessary steps and changes. The need of the hour now is to render necessary ways without being audacious for the harmonious development in the future. Prime care is needed for pin-pointing the faults causing damage of the development of tourism which should be acknowledged and corrected. Research on tourism should be conducted as research will present the problems and their remedies. On other words, the true purpose of tourism should be identified the unwanted effects of tourism and introduce the methods of remedy. It is vexed problem considered now that the rapidly expanding tourism industry be purged of its negative effects. Tourism values in upkeeping the socio-economic development, improving international understanding and facilities will continue to depend upon whether or not it can be controlled with sufficient intelligence to contain its damaging influence. But the adequate economic and legal provisions will have to be created in the country which can embed investment confidence among private sector investors both foreign and domestic. Main infrastructural facilities like electricity and transportation, basic efforts should be taken by His Majesty's Government of Nepal, keeping eye on the negative consequences on the environmental damage of the country. Present moves made to safeguard the ecology of the country with the promotion of tourism, should be pursued with the fullest vigour. Tourism does provide profitable prospects for the national treasury, care need to be taken that this prosperous sector does not become the victim of over use.

With the creation of highest tourism bodies such as Tourism Council under the chairmanship of Prime Minister and Tourism Development Board, the highest tourism organisation of the country have been created. His Majesty's Government of Nepal has celebrate the visit Nepal Year, 1998. In order to increase the number of tourists to half a million and to develop infrastructures for the 21st century with the active participation of the private sectors boosting the economic development of the country. It is believed that the success and feature of this program largely depends on the participation and involvement of the private sector in a move to assist government initiatives. Visit Nepal' 98—a landmark process which has considered at a right moment with the highest tourism organisation on its sheering sheel to sheer Nepal's tourism theme "A sustainable habitat through sustainable tourism" and Nepal's international slogan "Visit Nepal'98—a world of its own, Cooperative planning by organisations-governmental as well as non-governmental with different responsibilities and at different levels of government could be seen at the past and which caused difficulties in arriving to a successful implementation. But a worthwhile basis of Tourism National Organisation, represented by Tourism Council and Tourism Board will have been established for ongoing cooperation of all sectors engaged in Tourism development for making investment substantial out of resources of time and money. Tourism policy commitment has always to meet the principles set by Tourism Policy, 1995 to emphasize the need for strategies to evaluate opportunity to exploit market and resources potential for achieving economic and social benefits.

Nepal had celebrated the visit Nepal Year 1998 as a nation wide campaign for the development and promotion of tourism. It aims at diversifying tourism products/resources by popularizing the country as a good touristic destinations and to increase the number of tourists visiting the country.

3

LEISURE AND HOLIDAY TOURISM

Catalogue of Nepal's tourist attractions are many and varied. It has wide and varied set of geographical divisions, comprising from the tropical southern lowlands to the arctic Himalayan plateau. Between these regions are the Middle Hills, at whose breast lies the valley of Kathmandu, the traditional centre of Nepali culture and history.

DIFFERENT TOURIST ATTRACTIONS

No account of full catalogue of Nepal's tourist attractions has yet been catalogued, even so, same of the attractions given below assert proof of its greatness.

SCENIC AND RECREATIONAL AREAS

These resources cover Kathmandu valley—cultural centre, Excursion places, Pokhara—Lakes, trekking tour base, Central Hill—Tansen, Gorkha—look out points for viewing Himalayan snowy ranges, Western Hills—Jumla, Rara (blue Lake at 4087m), Eastern Hills—Dhankuta, Namche Bazar Solu Khembu and Everest areas. Really, Nepal conjures spectacular landscape—vision of world's highest mountains with snow - fed rivers running through green valleys.

HISTORIC MONUMENTS

The principal historic monuments in Nepal are temples, shrines and palaces located in the Kathmandu Valley. Most of these cultural treasures date from the late fifteenth to the eighteenth century. There are three types of temples—the pagoda—Nyatapol temple in Bhadgaon and Changu Narain at Changu being the best example, the Stupa—The biggest being those of Boudhanath and Swayambhunath and the Shikhara—the temple of Krishna Mandir in Patan. There are many historic cultural centres in other parts of the country. The temple of Pashupatinath in Kathmandu, Lumbini, the nativity of Siddhartha Gautam Buddha, Janakpur—birth place of Sita, the Consort of God Rama, the epic hero of Hindu epic Ramayana are of outstanding example.

Nepal is the cultural museum where art treasures and monuments of historical interest such as Durbar Square Complex of Kathmandu, Patan and Bhadgaon are preserved, Kathmandu with Patan and Bhadgoan second and third cities in importance constitute a rare ensemble of an architecture of great originality and quality. Innumerable temples both pagodas and stupas and many kinds of other interesting monuments and private houses with carved doors, balconies and windows testify to the rich cultural tradition which inspire the people to create and embellish them. It is believed to be as many as 3,000 temples in Kathmandu Valley.

Nepal is a land of cultural past which is enshrined in many a magnificent monuments. The major historic monuments in Nepal are temples and religious shrines, located in the Kathmandu Valley.

Kathmandu Valley cradle of Nepali culture and civilisation is the largest valley in the Midlands and certainly the most beautiful. The Kathmandu valley covers an area of 218 sq. miles. It is situated at 1310 m. above the sea level. The valley holds a great wealth of artistic and cultural treasures within its singular setting framed by the surrounding green hills and snow-capped peaks in the distant horizon. Art treasures along with religious as well as cultural resources are of an astonishing richness in the valley of Kathmandu. So there are seven World Heritage Sites (Cultural) are proclaimed by the United Nations Educational Scientific and Cultural Organisation (UNESCO) as World Heritage Sites within 20 kms. of radius which really speaking one of the few countries in the world having such a cultural sites so near to each other. These World Heritage Sites (cultural) are given below for information:

—Swayambhu Nath Stupa

—Boudha Nath Stupa

—Bhaktapur City

—Changunarain Temple

—Pashupatinath Temple

—Kathmandu Durbar Square

—Patan Durbar Square

So, Kathmandu valley is without question exotic due to its scenic attractions together with its cultural resources in the world.

ART AND CRAFTS

Nepal's traditional artistic skills are best demonstrated on the bronze sculptures, wood and stone carvings of the temples, Durbar Square Complexes and other places. The golden door of Bhadgaon is an illustrative display of Nepali art and crafts. Examples of the masterpieces of arts and crafts are found on each of the three cities of Kathmandu Valley.

FLORA AND FAUNA

The Terai lowland in the South possess a wide range of wildlife —elephant, rhinoceros, buffalo, tiger, leopard, bear, bison, deer and monkeys. The midlands are less rich in wildlife having bear and deer in their possession. The lower slopes of the Himalayas house the Himalayan bear, serow, Ghoral, Monal - Nepal National Bird, while the uninhabited valleys of the Himalayas shelter musk deer and many other species of flora and fauna.

Nepal is nature lover's paradise. In the Terai - Sal (Sorea Robusta) Sissau, Acacia grow in abundance. The inner Terai forests are full of Savannah with tall grassland and bamboo. In the middle Himalayan Zone or the hill country zone where pines, rhododendrons, elms, poplars, walnuts and willow grow in plenty. In the inner Himalayas—oaks, maples and pines flourish and in the alpine are junipers, short rhododendrons and variety of medicinal plants.

Nepal is also a repository of many species of birds, fishes reptiles - amphibians and insects. About 830 species of birds such as pheasants, snow pigeon, snow partridge, golden eagle etc. are noticed here.

National Parks and wildlife reserves have been established in different region of the country to view different varieties of wildlife in their natural habitat.

CULTURAL ACTIVITIES

Nepal is the land of colourful festivals. It is said that nearly 30 major festivals take place in Kathmandu Valley each year. All these festivals whether local or national character are religious in nature being associated with one of the divinities of Hindu or Buddhist mythology. All festivals are commonly celebrated by all people and this spectacular costumes and parades are of great interest.

HIMALAYAN PEAKS AND LANDSCAPES

Nepal's enigma is fairly established in her mountains. Most majestic attraction is snowy Nepal Himalayan peaks and romantic landscapes. Physically, it presents an attractive grandeur. The northern fringe is dotted with the highest peaks in the world. Mount Everest (8848 m) the world's highest peak dominates the amphitheater of numerous Himalayan peaks and tiers of hills. The grandeur of landscape has given the country a mystical charm of its own. Nepal, a valuable treasure house of visual delights offers a sightseeing through magnificent hills, valleys and lakes amidst breathtaking view of snowy Himalayan massifs Everest Dhaulagiri, Ama Dablam, Kanchanjunga, Annapurna etc.

In all, Nepal is a land of varied attractions for exotic

pleasures as well as for experiencing some of the greatest sites of South Asia's cultural heritage.

PLACES OF TOURIST INTEREST

Nepal has within its small territorial compass, vast natural attractions, places of cultural interests and singular fauna and flora. Its places of interest are so bewitching that they supply the picture of attractive vividness consisting of ruged mountain ranges, green cool and fertile valleys, tropical forests, alluvial land of the Terai with deep tropical vegetation, the panorama of massive Himalayan snows and the temples, stupas, historical monuments of rich artistic significance in Kathmandu Valley.

KATHMANDU

The Kathmandu valley with its tri-cities-Kathmandu, Patan and Bhadgaon can be called an open air museums. There cities are full of historical monuments, temples, stupas and many other places of cultural and artistic heritage. The Kathmandu valley is surrounded by green hills and mountains with snow-caped peaks along its northern and eastern horizons. The beautiful view of glittering pagodas, temples, white edifices and red hamlets seen in a romantic setting of hill and dale remains an ineffable memory. Kathmandu, the capital of the Kingdom of Nepal lies in the heart of the valley. It length from east to west is about 20 miles and its breadth from north to south about 15. It is situated at an altitude of 1336 meter above the sea level at the confluence of the two rivers—the Bagmati and the Bisnumati in wide valley.

The Kathmandu city is also known as Kantipur by its ancient name which means the city of beauty. In shape it resembles the sword of Devi (Goddesses). It is said to have been founded by Raja Gunkama Deva in 723 A.D. Durbar Square of Kathmandu with its old temples and palaces epitomises a grand show-piece of architecture. Important sight-seeing places in Kathmandu city are given below:

Hanuman Dhoka—The image of Hanuman is front of Hanuman Dhoka Palace main entrance was established by the

Malla King Pratap malla in 1672 A.D. The principal gate to the palace is guarded by the Monkey God (Hanuman) to scare away evil spirits in 1699 A.D. Since then, it has been called Hanuman Dhoka. King Pratap Malla built Nasala-Chowk and put in it Narasimha and Nrityanatha to which afterwards added various others. He built Indrapur and Jagatnath temple in front of Durbar in 1654 A.D. He composed a prayer to Kalika and had it inscribed on stone in fifteen different characters. He made a beautiful image of Nrityanath and placed it in a large temple which was named Madu-Nasala-Deva. He made a metal image of Biswarupa and placed outside the Durbar for worship. All traditional royal ceremonies are held in its courtyards.

Taleju Mandir—A Pagoda temple was built by the king Mahendra Malla in 1564 A.D. The temple is very high in the form of a Jantra (charm or Amulet). This is reckoned as one of the imposing pagoda temple in Nepal. A Pagoda having three storied is constructed on a big base with staircases around it. This is one of the most aesthetically pleasing structures in the Durbar complex. This is lofty and truely unique and every part of it is ornamented with exquisite wood carving, rich metal works and a range of sculpture.

Kumari Chowk—Near the Durbar Square lies the temple of living Goddess (Vestal Virgin) with profusely carved wooden balconies and windows. This temple built in 1757 by king Jaya Prakash Malla. It is the place where Kumari, the living Goddess resides. This temple of a three storeyed structure is decorated with carved pillars all around the courtyard. The living Goddess, chosen by the priests out of a Sakya clan, who lives in the temple until she attains a womenhood. Sometimes the Kumari can be seen appearing behind the latticed bay window. At the time of the grand Indra Jatra festival, she emerges from the temple and goes in a procession through the throughfare of the city to receive homage from the people. But photography is strictly prohibited.

Basantpur Durbar—This complex built by King Prithvi Narain Shah, the great, forefather of the present Shah rulers. It is full of carved roof struts, windows with intricate carvings and rises a full nine storeys with towers on its four sides with most imposing look and design.

Kasthamandap—Literary, the meaning of the building means a wooden shrine. A pagoda structure was constructed by king Laxmi Narsingh Malla in 1596 from the wood of a single tree. A three-storeyed building is consecrated to Gorakhnath by putting the image in the centre and an image of Ganesh at the four corners. It is also famous by the name of Maru Sattal. Kathmandu has deserved its name from it.

The Great Bell—The great bell was erected by King Rana Bahadur Shah in 1787 to scare away the evil spirits. There is a practice to ring the bell when worship is offered to Degutaleju.

The Great Drums—Two great drums were made during the time of rule of Girbana Yuddha Bikrama Shah in 1799-1816. These drums are played during the worship of Degutaleju.

The Image of Kala Bhairab—The collosal image of Bhairab was set by the King Pratáp Mall which represents Shiva in his destructive manifestation. It is said that this large image sculptured out of a single block of stone are famous all over the country.

Machchhendranath Temple—The pagoda temple of Machchhendranath is also rich in artistic beauty. This temple was made by the King Yaksha Malla in 1502 A.D. Later on, King Pratap malla introduced the annual festival of white Machchhendra Nath. The temple is situated in Indra Chowk on the way to Asan.

Akash Bhairab Temple—This temple is also situated in Indra Chowk. The idol of Akash Bhairab is displayed out of the temple for a week during Indra Jatra festival honouring rain God.

Dharahara—This is a tower measuring 50.5 meter constructed by Prime Minister Bhimsen Thapa in 1832. This tower is one of the imposing monuments in Nepal.

Narayanhity Royal Palace— This is the Royal Palace. At the southern main entrance to the palace, there is a historic water tank "Narayanhity" and a temple of Narayan which is also a gem of the sikhara style of architecture.

Singha Durbar—It is the imposing edifice with over 1600 rooms by a formal gardens. It was built by the late Rana Prime Minister Chandra Shumsher Jung Bahadur Rana as a private residence of Prime Minister. It is quite lavish and modern. It now houses the central secretariat of His Majesty's Government of Nepal.

Martyr's Memorial—The memorial contains the effigies of the martyrs who sacrified their lives in the revolution of 1950-51 for democracy against the Rana family rule.

Nepal's capital city, Kathmandu fuses old and modern atmosphere. The famed palace complex, temples and stupas epitomise the rich cultural heritage and ensemble of all of them is a fascinating combination of my architectural styles. The picturesque city is known for its modern glamour mingling with glorious past. Other places of interests in Kathmandu city is the twisting alleyways and streets of the old city full of market places with busy life, the Deshe Maru Jhya (only one window all over the country), Yettka Bahal, Itam Bahal, Naradevi, numismatic museum at Hunuman Dhoka and also temples of many gods and goddesses. Kathmandu is the metropolitan city of Nepal. This city was extended to its present shape in the early eighth century.

PATAN

Patan, the "City of beauty" as its ancient name Lalitpur signifies, is believed to have been constructed in 299 A.D. during the reign of Vera Deva. The city is circular in shape and is situated three kilometres south-east of Kathmandu, a short distance from the southern bank of the river Bagmati. The main Durbar Squre is located in the centre of the city. It is a city full of Buddhist monuments and Hindu shrines. It has always been famous for its craftsmen, masons, wood casters, silver and metal workers which can be appreciated by watching the artistic masterpieces in the many temples and monuments which are scattered everywhere in Patan. This city is full of Buddhist monuments, Hindu temples with five bronze gateways, guardian deities and endless carvings.

Durbar Square—This is an ancient seat of royalty of Malla Kings. Durbar Square is a store house of Buddhist monuments, Hindu Temples, fine brazen gateways and some of the most elaborate carvings. It is full of architectural objects such as old place complex, golden window, temple of Taleju, Tushahity—ancient royal bath etc. There are many beautiful temples at the courtyard of palace. The Golden Statue of Raja Yog Narendra Malla was created in front of Degutale temple by King Yog Narendra Malla and placed on it his son's statue. The golden window was built by Shri Vishnu Malla having a golden image of Aryavaloketeswara producing Brahma and other Gods. Tushahity or Royal Path with intricate carvings all around was made by King Siddhi Nar Singh Malla. The whole square is a cluster of fine pagoda temples and stone statues. The ancient palace and the temple complex of the medieval Malla Kings and the focal point of Patan's many cultural attractions.

Hiranya Varna Mahavihar—It is a unique Buddhist Monastery of three storeyed golden pagoda with a fine figure of Lokeshwar (Lord Buddha). It is built in the 12th century by King Bhaskar Varma, and is situated in the courtyard of Kwabahal. There are many decorations on its walls of very intricate nature. The shrine enshrines on a grand pedastal, the huge image of Buddha and a big 'Prayer wheel'. Many scenes epitomising the life of Buddha are painted and carved on its walls by master artists of bygone ages.

Kumbheswar Temple—This temple is dedicated to Lord Shiva and is a five storeyed pagoda style temple. Inside the courtyard, there is a mineral spring which is believed to have connection with the famous glacial lake of Gosainkunda. This temple was built by King Jayestheti Malla in 1422 A.D. Festivities and Mala held in Janai Purnima Day.

Jagat Narayan Temple—A tall picturesque temple of Lord Vishnu is made of red brick on the bank of Sankhamul river. There are images of Ganesh and Hanuman of artistic values in stone and a beautiful metal statue of Garuda on a stone pillar.

Krishna Mandir—Among the most beautifully decorated temple is Krishna Mandir which features a number of episodes from the Ramayana and Mahabharata epics. This temple was built by King Siddhi Narsingh Malla in 16th century. This is full of intricate details and scenes from Epics Ramayana and Mahabharat which are engraved in stone. The style of temple is most perfect and provides an illustrations example of the Nepali temple craft. This is Shikhara Style temple.

Mahaboudha—This unique temple was built around the 14th century by Abhaya Raj, a priest of Patan. This is the fine example of the use of Terracotta in architecture. Every brick of this temple is embossed with the image of Buddha and so it is called the temples of a million Buddhas.

Rudra Varna Mahavihar—This is a Buddhist monastery near Mahaboudha temple. There are many fine figures all around it. There is a temple near it with a fine figure of Lord Buddha. Besides these, there are art works of different figures made of bronze and stone.

Red Machchhendranath Temple—This temple was considered to have built in 1408 A.D. This is also a pagoda styled temple which is located in a big quadrangular square. There are numerous works of fine arts of different figures made of bronze around this temple. Avaloketeshwar or Red Machchhendranath is housed here for six months a year and then the image is taken round the city of Patan in a colourful chariot festival in April-May. This temple is gorgeous with the decorations and is largely due to the immense amount of silver leaf used in gilding.

Minnath Temple—A small but picturesque pagoda. It lies just opposite the Machendra Nath Temple. This temple is also full of carvings and decorations.

Ashokan Stupas—There are four stupas at four corners of Patan. It is said that these stupas were created during Indian Emperor Ashok's pilgrimage to Kathmandu Valley. This gives the city a monastic look. These Buddhist mounds were built in 250 A.D.

Patan Industrial Estate—There are many small industrial complex for manufacturing metal furnitures, carpets, screens, bamboo artworks, metal and semi-precious orgaments etc. are housed here.

Zoo—Jawalakhel Zoo has some of the finest specimens of Himalayan fauna. This place is also good for picnicking and holidaying.

The Tibetan Camp—This camp is situated on the outskirts of Patan. The Tibetan people living there has established several sourvenir shops producing authentic Tibetan crafts such as prayer wheels of wood, ivory, silver or bronze, long temple horns made of beaten copper, buckles and jewellery. This is a good place to observe the process of weaving carpets by hands by the Tibetans.

BHAKTAPUR

It is located fifteen kilometres east of Kathmandu and the living museum of Nepali rich art and architecture. Bhaktapur, also known as Bhadgaon is another city of the Kathmandu Valley. It is ancient city with repository of Nepali culture. It has full of numerous temples, palaces, statues and other arts of a glorious past. The city is the store house of Nepali medieval art and architecture. It is regarded as the oldest town of the valley. It had origin in the time of the Lichhavi ruler. Later in 889 A.D., it was expanded in the shape of a conch shell an emblem of the Hindu God Vishnu by the King Ananda Deva. It is located at an altitude of 1,402 meters above sea level. Bhaktapur means the "city of devotees" and its traditional arts are pottery and weaving. These are the places worth seeing—

Siddha Pokhari—This is a big historic water tank near Bhaktapur city gate built by Raja Bhupatendra Malla. The

Himalayan ranges can be seen from here in all their majestic beauty in clear days.

Durbar Square—The main centre of the city presents innumerable temple and other architectural showpieces in the courtyard of its palace complex. The architectural pieces such as the lion gate, the picture Gallery, the Golden Gate, the palace of 55 windows, the statue of King Bhupatendra Malla, Batsala temple and the Pashupati temple are considered a masterpieces of Nepali art and architecture.

The Lion Gate—The gate is adorned with the lovely stone figures of Hanuman, Bhairawa and Narashingha. There are two big figures of lions on either side of the gate as guardians.

The Golden Gate—This golden gate dates from the reign of King Ranjit Malla in 1756 A.D. It is famous as the richest piece of art in the whole country. It is the entrance to the 55 window palace and many intricate figures of different lizards and designs are placed in a handsome setting.

The Palace of Fifty Five Windows—The ancient palace is remarkable for its carved balcony with 55 windows. This was built by King Yaksha Malla in 1427 A.D. It is constructed of bricks, elaborately carved and decorated with wooden window frames and doorways.

The Picture Gallery—It is full of tapestries ranging from Hindu and Buddhist School of Trantricism.

The Statue of King Bhupatendra Malla—This statue is very famous for its arts in column. It is erected by King Yaksha Malla in 1427 A.D.

The Big Bell—This is the biggest bell in the whole country.

Batsala Temple—This is a very beautiful temple full of artistic decorations. It is noted for "Bell of Barking Dogs." The sound of which is said to be the exact reproduction of the sound of death. When the bell rings, the local dogs commence barking and howling. This temple is made of stone with fine sculptural designed of gods and goddess around it. It is dedicated to

Goddess Batsala Devi and is designed after the shikhara style of architecture on top of a carved stone staircases.

Pashupati Temple—This temple is a replica of the famous Pashupati Nath Temple of Kathmandu. It is full of wood carving and erotic pictures. King Jitendra Malla renovated this temple in 1682 A.D. This temple is full of erotic carvings.

Nytapola Temple—This temple is erected at the time of Raja Bhupatendra Malla in 1708 A.D. This five storied temple stands on a five tiered platform with figures of men, elephants, lions, griffins and deities perched on each other. This is the best specimen of pagoda architecture in Nepal. The wooden frame work which bears the rafters of the roof is also very decorative in a harmonious proportions. The temple is guarded by five pairs of strange figures.

Bhairava Nath Temple—It is magnificently constructed on a gigantic scale. It was first erected in one storied type pagoda temple at the time of King Jagat Jyoti Malla and later elevated by King Bhupatendra malla in 1708 A.D. and placed Bhairava for the protection of the country. The chariot festival of Bhairava was also introduced by King Jagat Jyoti Malla on the eve of Mesh Sankranti (summer solstice) when a tall pole is erected in his honour as a flagstaff.

Dattatraya Temple—It is said that this temple was built from the trunk of a single tree. This temple was built by King Yaksha Malla and repaired by Biswa Malla in 1458 A.D. This temple is dedicated to Lord Shiva.

Near this temple, there is a lane going to the Math (Monastery) of the temple with exquisitely carved windows. The famous peacock window is also there with its superleading art. It was carved in the reign of Biswa Malla in 1458 A.D. The Peacock window and its minute carving represent a peacock in full pride which is bold and well-executed.

Wakupati Narayan—This temple was built in 1632 A.D. It is very richly ornamented temple. It is a lovely specimen of the art of metal work.

Temple of Tulaja Bhawani—The temple of Bhawani is very ancient. It was built by King Hari Singha Deva in 1324 A.D. He enshrined the Goddess in a temple which he named Mula-Chowk. The golden temple of Sri and Laxmi are on two side of the main gateway to the temple of Taleju. There are golden spires and umbrella on the roof. There is a sandalwood window which is considered to be carved by King Bhupatendra Malla himself to please the Goddess.

PLACES OF ATTRACTIONS AROUND KATHMANDU VALLEY

Set against the backdrop of Nepal Himalaya in the distant horizon, Kathmandu valley is a land of exceptional scenery and a fascinating people and culture. Kathmandu valley is a cultural museum where art treasures of monuments of historical and religious interest are preserved. The arts and crafts of Nepal, inspired by ancient Buddhist and Hindu culture are of an astonishing richness in the Kathmandu Valley. An abundance of temples, stupas, monasteries and Durbar complex of tri-cities of Kathmandu Valley makes the country, a land of devotees who keep alive a deep religious heritage. The combination of temples and stupas, the artistic creations of man silhouetted against the background of natural charm, furnishes to Nepal a spell and individuality which is marvellous and distinct. The places of attractions around Kathmandu Valley given below assert proof of their greatness. The valley alrounds in cultural and glorious legends and covers an area of 218 sq. miles.

Balaju Water Garden—This is situated at the foot of Nagarjuna hill, 4 kms. north-west of Kathmandu. There are 22 dragon headed water spouts. Balaju is famous by the name of water garden, designed beautifully in a new park in an old historic place. There is also sculpture of Lord Vishnu (replica of Budhanilkantha) lying recumbent on a small water tank. There are several ponds full of fishes. It has also a newly built olympic size swimming pool. Nearby lies the Balaju Industrial District.

Swayambhunath Stupa—West to Balaju water garden, Swayambhunath, a sacred Buddhist stupa is on the top of a hillock overlooking a good panorama of the Kathmandu city and the snowy mountains. One of the oldest stupa in Nepal, it is reputed to be of 2,000 years old. The main features of the stupa is the hemispherical solid dome, the conical construction painted with the all seeing eyes of Lord Buddha and the 15 ring bronze spire topped off by an umbrella. It is full of numerous miniature votive stupas. Swayambhunath, the stupa of the primordial Buddha, self-arisen and uncreated represents. Avaloketeshvara, the very embodiment of compassion. It is three kilometre west of Kathmandu.

The National Museum—It is famous for its collection of Nepalese and Tibetan arts, stone sculptures, paintings, wood carvings, bronze works and ancient and medieval war weapons of Nepal etc. Among the historical artifacts are the sword of Louis Napolean and the leather cannon from Tibet.

Boudhanath—The biggest Buddhist stupa is considered to have been built by King Man Deva. This stupa is about 30° yards in circumference. The solid dome of stupa is surmounted by a bronze minaret of peculiar shape on a circular platform. These are niches around the platform each of which is filled with a roll of Buddhist player wheels and the devotees turn the cylinders as they walk around the stupa. It is situated at eight kilometers east of Kathmandu. It is thought to be the highest stupa on the world.

Gokarnaban-Wildlife Santuary—It is about two miles north-east of Pashupatinath temple on the Bagmati river. There is an ancient temple of Gokarneswar, renovated by King Jayastheti Malla in about 1422 A.D. This is also famous place for picnic. It contains a wild life santuary very near from the Kathmandu city. Wild life viewing can be done. It is 64 acres of preserved forests. The spotted deer, sambar, barking deer, wild boar, civet, leopard and monkeys can be seen.

Sundarijal—This is a ideal place for excursion and picnic. This place is really lovely after the monsoon season as it bounds with the spectacular cascading waterfalls, cataracts and rivulets with lush green vegetations and beautiful landscape. This is also an ideal place for camping and resting. This place is located 13 kilometres north-east of the Kathmandu city at the foothills surrounding valley.

Kirtipur—This ancient township is situated on the top of a plateau. This is a very ancient town of Nepal with many kinds of typical attractions. People are seen here in their typical life style and in their age-old costumes. Tribhuwan University lies at the base of the town. The panorama of Kathmandu Valley can be seen from the town with snowy peaks in the background. It is situated about 8 km. south-west of Kathmandu and typical village town preserving the old tradition.

Shankhu—This is situated in the old town. This place is known for the Temple of Bajrayogini which is dedicated to the Goddess of Tantricism. The temple is very beautiful amidst green environment. The landscape is very attractive and also atmosphere. This temple is very ancient. It is made in pagoda style and the roof is of golden colour.

Chovar—This is located 4 miles south-east of Kathmandu. It is said that once Kathmandu Valley was a lake and Manjushree, a sage made a sword cut to drain out Kathmandu Valley. On the hill top, there is a small pagoda temple of Adinath. Magnificent views of snow-clad peaks can be seen on clear days. This place is really marvellous after the monsoon rains.

Pharping and Dakshinkali—Both these places are famous for Hindu pilgrimage. A lovely countryside drive of approximately 25 km. south west of Kathmandu, Dakshin Kali, is one of the famous shrines of the mighty mother goddess of the Hindu amidst green pine woods. The sacrifice of duck, goat, cock and buffalo can be made to the goddess for appeasement. An hour's scenic drive from the Kathmandu city, Daksinkali is a famous Hindu temple for sacrifice particularly on Tuesday and Saturday. Magnficent view of the surrounding landscape is marvellous.

One way to the shrine of Dakshinkali, there is Pharping which has a beautiful shrine of Shekhar Narayan. These are also ponds with different kinds of fishes in the courtyard of the shrine. Shekhar Narayan or Shesh Narayan Temple is about 14 km. south and Kathmandu on way to Daksinkali shrine. It is a forested area with tall beautiful trees.

Guheswori Temple—This is the shrine of Goddess Parvati, Lord Shiva's consort. The architecture of this temple is quite unique as it is in a form of Tantric design and concept. Only Hindu are allowed to go inside the courtyard.

Pasupatinath Temple—This is the most imposing pagoda styled temple and one of the most famous places of Hindu pilgrimage in the world. The temple is dedicated to Lord Shiva—the guardian deity of Nepal. This holy place is picturesque collection of temple and shrines. This temple is a handsome pagoda with a golden gild roof and large richly carved silver gates. All the dying persons are brought to Pasupatinath for cremation. Only the Hindus are allowed to go inside the temple.

PLACES OF ATTRACTIONS OUTSIDE THE KATHMANDU CITY

Nepal has much to offer from the snow-capped Himalayas to the cultural resources within its small campass. In short, variety is the true delight of Nepal Travel. Diversity forms attractions and exotic pleasures as well as for experiencing some of the greatest sites of South Asia's cultural heritage. It is a valuable treasure house of visual delight which offer a wide range of unforgettable natural panorama, historical places, traditional artistry and the rich cultural heritage. The major place of attractions outside the Kathmandu Valley are given below:

1. Nagarkot—Situated 32 kilometres east of Kathmandu at an altitude of 2195 meters, this spot is the most scenic place in Bhaktapur district. It provides a vantage point for viewing the sunrise over Everest, the highest peak of the world. Stunning Himalayan views, with the terraced fields and thatched houses of mid-country Nepal spread out before you.

This lovely hill resort stands between Kathmandu valley in the west and the Indravati river valley in the east. The climate of this resort is salubrious and the scenery is magnificent. From here, the major peaks of the eastern Nepal Himalaya can be seen. Treks from Nagarkot are unique and delightful. The trekker comes near to the wonderful scenery, flower covered meadows and many unusual rock formations. The beautiful sun rise or sun set view on the Nepal Himalayas can be enjoyed by staying in one of the accommodation there.

2. Dhulikhel—It is a anciet township located 30 kilometres east of Kathmandu joining the Arniko Raymarg (Kathmandu-Kodari Highways). The majestic view of the whole Himalayan range from west to east can be seen from the spot. One can see the surrounding countryside of its terraced hills and a undulating topography of lowlands and towering peaks.

PLACES OF INTERESTS OUTSIDE THE VALLEY

3. Namobuddha—It is situated on a trail for trek from Dhulikhel. It is famous for stupas of Namobuddha. The legend of Namobuddha tells that prince went hunting in the area and saw tigers with her cubs searching for foods. Being compassion for them, the prince cut his own flesh and gave to the tigers and the cubs. Later on he was also devoured by the tigers. A memorial depicted the same in the site of sacrifice. The prince was regarded as the reborn Buddha. This is also a monastery near by.

4. Panauti—This is a holy place located in the confluence of the Rose and Punyamatta rivers. These are many pagoda style temples built in 15th century. There are smaller stone Dharmasalas. In the month of Magh (mid-January), a large number of pilgrims come here to celebrate in the festival of Magha Sankranti. The people also congregate here in the bank of the river once every twelve years to take a holy bath.

Budhanilkantha—This holy place is located eight kilometers north of Kathmandu. There is a big courtyard and a big pond.

The big pond is covered with a huge stone idol of recumbent Vishnu on a bed of serpants (Naga) and the head resting under its nine-headed hood. At the food of the Seopuri hill, this holy place is containing the tank and the collosal image of Nilkantha Narayan. The image is considered to be constructed in the seventh century A.D. This is a 18 ft. long sleeping image of God Vishnu, the "God of protection" lying here on a bed of snakes "Anantashesha". It is famous place of pilgrimage for Hindus.

Godavari—It is situated six miles south of Patan. It is a good picnic spot amidst thick wooded jungle. Here is fish hatchery, marble mine. St. Xavier's School, agricultural farm. There is also Royal Botanical garden. It is one of the holiest places in Nepal and once every twelve years a great number of pilgrims come from all parts of Nepal to have a holy bath in the tank. There are many shrines and tanks picturesquely situated at the foot of the hill.

Bajra Barahi—The temple of Barahi (Incarnation of Vishnu in the form of a Boar) is situated in wooded place. It is about ten kilometres south of Patan city and is linked by road. One can enjoy charm of rural life and natural landscapes by driving up to Tika Bhairab. There are many old but interesting villages are Sonaguthi, Chapagaon on the way.

Phulchoki—This is the name of a hill, approximately 20 km. southeast of Kathmandu at an altitude of 2758 m is thickly covered with green trees, rhododendrons and wild roses bloom at the way to the top in varying colours. This place is good for hiking and camping. There is also a small shrine at the top of the hill. One can view magestic view of the Himalayas, Kathmandu valley and also the southern Terai plains on a clear day.

Suryavinayak—This is the temple of Ganesh (Elephant God). It is situated in the loveliest setting in sylvan atmosphere. The temple looks very beautiful amidst natural foliage of magnificent evergreen trees. The view of ancient city of Bhaktapur from here is worth seeing.

Changunarayan—This is believed to be the oldest pagoda temple of the valley, artistic heritage of the Lichavian era. It is an ancient historical place situated at an altitude of 153 m. It is located on the hill named Kileswara and there is a composite image representing Lokeshwar upon Vishnu, Garuda and a lion. The temple was built by Vishnu Gupta and later improved by Hari Datta. The temple is richly decorated with sculpture and carvings. It is about 15 km. east of Kathmandu.

Pasupatinath—This is the most glorious pagoda temple and one of the most famous places of Hindu pilgrimage in the world. It preserves the gorgeous original style of pagoda architecture of times before the 6th century. The temple is dedicated to Lord Shiva, the guardian deity of Nepal. This holy place is a picturesque collection of temples and shrines. This temple is about five kilometres east of Kathmandu city with a golden gilt roof and large richly carved silver gates. All the dyings are brought to Pasupatinath for cremation. It is on the banks of the sacred Bagmati river.

The Hindus are allowed to go inside the court of the temple. Non-Hindus can view this magnificent temple from the eastern side, across the Bagmati river.

5. Kodari Border—The road to Chinese border links Kathmandu with the autonomous region of Tibet region of the People's Republic of China. It is 115 km. north-east of Kathmandu on the way, scenery of sylvan countryside and landscapes.

6. Palanchawk Bhagawati—This is a small village situated 6 miles east of Panchkhal on the Chinese built highway to Kodari. From Panchakhal a track of 2 hours is required to reach the top where there is a temple of Bhagawati of fifth century. The hill top is a good place to view the Himalayas. A good place is recommended for short trekking.

7. Kakani—It is about 29 km. north-west of Kathmandu at an altitude of 1982 m. and famous for is landscapes and panoramic view of Nepal Himalayas such as Annapurna,

Ganesh Himal and Himalchuli etc. It stands between the Kathmandu valley in the south-east and Trisuli river valley in the north-west. This is also a hill resort with a sylavan beauty. This place offers natural beauty of supreme grandeur in the lake winter when the trees growing in the full slopes begin to bloom. The sun-rise and sun-set view of the majestic Himalayan peaks can be enjoyed by staying overnight in the rest houses there. It is connected by motorable road. Kakani provides look right into face of the Ganesh Himal Gaurishanker and Manaslu standing right in front to you. This is quiet forest walks.

PLACES OF INTERESTS IN THE WEST AND EAST PART OF THE COUNTRY

8. **Pokhara**—The enchanting lake distinct of Pokhara panoramic valley is linked with Kathmandu by road about 200 kilometers as well as regular flight of Royal Nepal Airlines and other private airlines. This is the secondary tourist destination after Kathmandu valley and is one of the most picturesque sports in Nepal. It is situated above sea level and is connected by a highway (Prithvi Rajmarga) with Kathmandu. Siddhartharajmarga links it with midland valley and Terai through the most beautiful natural landscapes, Pokhara valley is a jewel amidst a mountain panorama. Against the stupendous backdrop of the Annapurna range with the majestic snow-capped Machhapuchhare in the foreground, the valley is filled with terraced fields, lakes, rivers and gorges. Dominating the lush green valley is the famous Machhapuchhare (fish-tail) peak which piers like the crown on the valley's brow. Besides the Himalayas other charms of the valley are its emerald lakes such as Fewa, Rupa and Begnas. Among them, Phewa Tal is the biggest lake and the reflection of the majestic Machhapuchhare peak on its bosom casts a magical spell. Boating and swimming on the lakes are organised. The Seti river flows very deep and many gorges of the enormous depth can be seen. This is the gateway for making hike and trekking. Angling is one of the best spots in Pokhara. There are many kinds of fishes in its cold water of the lakes and snow-fed rivers. Pony riding can also be enjoyed in its

natural world of pleasure. It consists of vergin forests and carpet like meadow in nature's most picturesque settings. Comfortable accommodations are available in Pokhara. A charming town with a dozen daytrips around.

In Pokhara valley, the mountain lover can view the prominent peaks from east to west are Annapurna South (7, 119 meters), Fang (7,6471 meters), Rock Noir (7,454 meters), Glacier Dome (7193 meters), Gangapurna (7,455 meters), Annapurna I (8,091 meters) Annapurna III (7,555 meters) Machhapuchhare (6,997 meters) and others. Daulagiri I to the north-west are also visiable.

In the island of Phewa lake, there is the famous temple of Barahi (Goddess Bhagavati). At Batulechaur, a cave lies for viewing of the stalactite and stalagmite rocks and this is famous as Mahendra Gupha. The Seti river has stroke of a narrow canyon having depth of 150 ft. to 250 ft. from the surface. The river is called Seti because of the faom and froth that is creates while squeezing headlong through the narrow gorge. Saurankot and Kaon Kot are the two best look-outs for viewing enchanting valley of Pokhara and snowy ranges. Trekking to many places such as Jomsom Tukuchhi Thak, Muktinath and Mustang can be done from here.

Tansen—It is an ancient town situated at an altitude of 1,371 meters on the slopes of Srinagar hill. It is a popular summer resorts of the western Nepal. It has salubrious climate. It is also full of artistic temples, shrines and stupas. This town looks like Kathmandu. The inhabitants of this town worship both Hindu and Buddhist Gods and Goddesses in a spirit of equal reverence.

Tansen is also a good place for making treks into the adjoining district of Palpa. There are travels such as Ridhi Rishikesh via Chandi Bhanjyang, Rani Ghat over the Chutre Bhanjyang and Ramji Ghat via Begnas. The majestic view of the city can be enjoyed in the upland Srinagar hill. It is joined by road from Pokhara and Siddharthanagar. A quiet hill town full of attractions with lakes, oaks, rhododendrons and an unparalled view from the southern Terai to the Himalayas.

Lumbini—This place is the sacred place for the Buddhist and the sacred pilgrimage site. Lumbini—the birthplace of Gautama, the Buddha lies in the alluvial plains 150 km. north-east of Kathmandu valley and south of the first foothills of the Himalayas, the Churia range. It lies in a very ancient place called Rupandehi dstrict in the Lumbini zone of Nepal. Sakya Muni Gautama Buddha was born at Rupandehi (also called Lumbini Garden. It is proved now by almost all historians and research scholars that Emperor Ashoka paid a visit to Lumbini in 249 B.C. A stone pillar installed at Lumbini of that age speaks of this royal visit of the emperor.

Gautama Buddha was born in Lumbini Park in 623 B.C. under a Sal Grove (Sorea Robusta) on the full moon day of the sixth month of the lunar calendar. He was born on the full moon day of Baishak Purnima and this day is the most important and pious day for the Buddhists. His birth enlightenment and emancipation (nirvana) were also on Baishak Purnima. This Baishak Purnima is also popular by the name of Buddha Purnima among the Buddhists in Nepal and all over the world.

Lumbini has been accounted along with Bodh Gaya, Sarnath and Kushinagar in India (the places of His enlightenment, first sermon, and emancipation (Nirvana) respectively as one of the four sacred places of pilgrimage. So it rises to an equal standing with the holy places dedicated to other world religions. Gautama Buddha proclaimed the glorious doctrine for the gain of the many, for the welfare of the many and in compassion for the world.

His Majesty's Government of Nepal has given high priority to the development of Lumbini. Limbini was in the remote places of south-western Nepal and it's isolation and lack of facilities make it as a difficult place to reach for devoted pilgrims. But the late secretary General U. Thant of the united Nations visited the sacred Garden Lumbini in 1967 and he called upon the international community to make it a prilgrimage and tourist centre. Thirteen nation International Lumbini Development Committee was formed in New York under the chairmanship of Nepal's permanent representative to the United Nations. In 1978, the Master Plan was finalised prepared by the world famous Japanese architect Professor Kenjo Tange. To-day the Lumbini Development Trust administers and coordinates the ongoing effort to restore Lumbini.

The places to visit in Lumbini is the ancient Maya Devi Temple and a sculpture of third century B.C. depicting the scene of the birth of Buddha. The Queen Maya Devi, the mother of Buddha stands holding the branch of a Sal tree. The birthplace of Lord Buddha one of the world's most important pilgrimage sites.

The Asokan Pillar—The Ashoka Maurya, the Emperor of India who ruled in the Third Century B.C. erected a tall monolith which still stands today, making mark the place where "the Buddha Sage of the Sakyas was born here".

Two Buddhist monasteries are also there and there are modern additions. The Tibetan-style monastery contains a huge image of Buddha and ancient morals decorate the walls of the both monasteries.

Besides these, there are ruined walls, a restored rectangular pond and some arounds.

Lumbini has now accommodation facilities. It is linked with the town of Siddharthnagar where there is an airport connected by regular flights from Kathmandu. There is also highway connection to Lumbini from Pokhara or Kathmandu via Narayanghat. Lumbini is also encluded as one of the World heritage sites by the United Nations Educational Scientific and Cultural Organisations (UNESCO) recently.

Janakpur—It is situated on the south-east of Kathmandu. It lies in the Mahottari district in the Terai Region of Nepal. This places famous for its marble temple of Janaki. Janakpur is an epic famed town and birth-place of Sita, wife of Rama, the hero of the epic Ramayana, and she got married with him here.

The marble temple of Janaki constructed by queen Vrisha Bhanu of the Indian state of Tikamgarh with the contribution of nine lakh (900,000 rupees) and so this temple is also known as Naulakha temple. Close to Janaki temple, there is another temple known as Rama Temple. These two temples become a centre of pilgrimage for the Hindus from all parts of Nepal and India in two main festivals Ram Nawami, Vivaha Punchami. Besides these temples, there are many sacred waterponds. Janakpur has now many hotels and it can be reached by plane or road from Kathmandu.

Biratnagar—It lies in eastern Terai region of Nepal in Kosi Zone. This is an industrial city. There are many industries here. A visit to Dharan and Barahachhetra is also interesting. Both these places are famous places of pilgrimage. It is connected with Kathmandu both by air and road.

Gorkha—This is the original home of the world famous Gorkha soldiers. It is a town situated in a hillock. The Great King Prithvi Narayan Shah was the King of Gorkha. He started the great integration compaign and finally succeeded in consolidating the whole of Nepal into a single country and nation. It is the ancestral home of Shah Dynasty.

There are two very famous temple of Gorakhnath and Kalika. It also contains the old Royal Palace of the King Prithvi Narayan Shah. In the eastern side, is the famous temple of Gorakhnath. The most famous pilgrimage spot of Manakamana is very near from here. The water fall at Namchi Danda falling down from 700 ft. can be viewed from the beautiful spot of Bar Pak of Gorkha. Gorkha is accessible by road from Kathmandu or Pokhara.

Daman—It is situated eighty kilometres south-west of Kathmandu. It can be reached by a picturesque highway known as Tribhuvan Rajpath linking Kathmandu with the Terai and Indian border. This is a highway full of scene and scenery. It commands an excellent views of Mt. Sagarmatha (Mount Everest) and the other high snow-capped Himalayan peaks. There is a view tower and a rest house.

Leisure and Holiday can be more lively exciting and memorable for tourists by becoming part of the spots and entertainment. They can prolong their stay and enjoy full moment getting involved in entertainments. The introduction of entertainments along with tourism has provided to be viable in the expansion of tourism industry. Tourists with interest visiting Nepal can enliven their stay by getting involved in one of the many sport events that the country offer.

ENTERTAINMENT

There are four Casinos in Kathmandu. Casino Nepal is the first casino in Nepal established in 1968 in Soaltee Hotel while Casino Anna situated at hotel de'l' Annapurna is the second one starting from 1992. Everest Casino situated in Everest Hotel Complex is the third one and the fourth one is the Casino Royale Complex at Hotel Yak and Yeti. All four casinoes run by the same management. There casinos open 24 hours throughout the week and provide indoor games and free transportation service from major hotels.

Cultural Entertainments

—The Everest Cultural Society next to the Hotel de'l Annapurna at Durbar marg, performs Nepali classical and folk dances every morning.

—New Himalchuli culture group at Hotel Shanker at Lazimpat features traditional ethnic dances and musical programmes daily from 7 to 8 p.m.

—Many cultural shows are also organised in various places now.

Parks and Zoo

—Jawalakhel Zoo. The only Zoo in Nepal houses exotic animals and bird species of South Asia. It has a rich collection of Himalayan fauna.

—Royal Botanical Garden at Godavari which is some 19 kilometers south-east of Kathmandu, contained a variety of exotic plant and flower species.

—Balaju Water Garden—Five kilometers, west of

Kathmandu features 22 Makara—headed water sports of the mid18th century and a public swimming.

—Gokarna Safari Park—10 km. east of Kathmandu city provides Elephant safari for viewing wild animals and other games.

Museums

—The National Museum near Swayambhunath houses early Nepali arts, historic items and ancient military weapons.

—The Tribhuvan Museum of Hanuman Dhoka gives a glimpse of the life of Late King Tribhuvan in pictures.

—The Museum of Natural History located near Swayambhunath houses a collection of different living species preserved in chemicals and taxidermic birds and butterflies.

—The National Art Museum housed in the old Malla Palace of Bhaktapur, displays ancient thanka arts and relics.

The Mountain Flight—Royal Nepal Airlines Corporation and other private airlines operate mountain flights. The flight takes the tourists quite close to the main Himalayan range. The plane flies alongside the mountains offering side and top views of almost all the peaks of the eastern Himalayan range including the world highest peaks, Mount Everest, Kanchanjunga and Makalu, fly over Himalaya for an hour.

Elephant Polo—There is water polo and horse polo and these games are popular. But Elephant polo is not so heard about and this polo is played in Nepal at the National Safari Park, Chitwan. This polo is played from a top of Elephant since 1981, Elephant polo is being played early year in December at Chitwan in the grassfield next to the Meghauli air-strip and is organised by Tiger Tops, Nepal. Now, it is called World Elephant Polo Championship. It is a five packed event. It is now getting popular by being participating from Nepal, Britain, Hongkong, U.S.A. and Germany. This Elephant polo is the game which is played only in Nepal not in any part of the world.

In A Nut Shell

Nepal is the land of infinite variety. The great Himalayan peaks across northern Nepal are topped by Mount Everest (8848 m). Mount Everest together with eight snow peaks of over 8000 m and about two hundred 4877 m mountains. Towards the West Nepal extends beyond the Himalayan range to the Trans-Himalayan area which is similiar of the Tibetan Plateau. The highest and most dramatic peaks lie to the North and in the eastern half of Nepal. The dramatic complex of snowy peaks of Nepal Himalaya and varied topography forms the basis of tourism attraction of Nepal. Set against the backdrop of the Nepal Himalayas lies a land of exceptional scenery and a fascinating people and culture. There is perpetual ice and snow above 4877 m altitude in Nepal and so it is a land of snow and milk-white dazzle. The highest and mightiest Himalayan peaks are viewed as nature's marvel, vast in unchallenged and isolated supremacy. The panorama of snow-capped peaks of Nepal is picturesque beyond of any country.

Nepal has a population of 20 million and are divided into numerous ethnic groups speaking different languages and dialects. But all the people whatever their race or tribal stocks peacefully co-exist and this character of the Nepali people has created an unique Nepali culture. Hinduism and Buddhism are both equally honoured in Nepal and the blending of the two religions into one entity have inspired and created the distinct culture of its own. The reflection of their uniqueness of the Nepali culture can be seen in the every day life of the people and the works of arts and architecture. There is religious tolerance everywhere. Everything is based on compromise and understanding. So the Nepali people and their way of life act as a major attraction to visitors and represent an important facet of cultural tourism.

Nepal is a most colourful country with active blend of Asian cultures. An abundance of temples, stupas, monasteries and Durbar complex of tri-cities of Kathmandu valley makes the country a land of devotees who keep alive a deep religious heritage. So far as the arts and architectures are concerned, Nepal is a lovelier place than thus the heart of man could scare desire. The beautiful scene of golden pagodas, temples, stupas. While edifices and red hemlets seen in a romantic background of hill and valley remain as ineffaceable memory. The prevalence of craftsmanship reflects the works of many craftsman continuing their arts over the centuries. And the way of life of people and festivities as common episodes dot the annual calender of Nepal with all sorts of colourful procession and rejoining.

The historical arts and architectures are the splendour of man made cultural values. Side by side with them, the wonderful flora and fauna of Nepal, and natural attractions of peaceful valleys and another splendours as natural values. Nepal is also botanically one of Asia's richest areas. The varied climate displays a unique variety of geographical regions, embracing an exceptional scenic beauty. It has tropical sub-tropical to alpine type of vegetation. But the most important point is that the spectacle whether natural, cultural or artistic that Nepal holds are such that they belong to a class by themselves, so refresingly different from elsewhere. Nepal dreams leisure and holiday tourism with excitement and novelty but relaxed enough to provide a visitor the magnificent scenery, rare wildlife, culture, arts and architectures and festivities as unforgetable sight.

4

CULTURAL AND PILGRIMAGE TOURISM

Nepal has within its small territorial boundary singular tourist attractions including various sites full of art and architectural show pieces in the background of natural panorama. It has a most favourable position and as such helds exiting fascination owing to the vastness of natural attractions, the high standard of cultural achievements, pleasant, coolness of its climate and uniqueness of its fauna and flora.

Nepal has the cultural and religious heritage as it has the combination of elements to attract the attention of visitors and provoke a visit by them. This combination represents the supply of Nepal Tourist Market. Nepal is not only a geological mosaic but also a human mosaic. There are many castes and creeds but no rigidity. Hinduism and Buddhism are equally honoured and the blending of the two religions in one entity has inspired and created the distinct culture of its own. There is religious tolerance everywhere. Basically the Nepal people are warm-hearted and hospitable. Everything is based on compromise and understanding. The reality of these uniqeness can be seen in the everyday life of the people and in the works of arts and architecture.

Religion has played an important role in moulding the outlook, attitude and ways of life of the people. It has given them a distinct cultural identity. One of them most remarkable elements to grasp in the Nepali people's way of life in their religion. Their religious fervour is indeed intense and devout and the religious tolerance has created heterogeneous ethnic and cultural elements into a remarkable fabric of distinctive character. The Nepali people belief in understanding each other and so have assimilated best ability to co-exist peacefully and live a happy life. They are proud of their tradition.

Attractive festivals both gay solemn are celebrated round the year. These festival are elegantly focused the traditional modes of Nepalese people. These festivals actually have inspired a calendar of events which reflect the rich culture and religious sentiments which are the heritage of an ancient culture.

The age-old cultural heritage of Nepal has helped to foster the growth of a splendid art, architecture and religious tradition. The art and crafts of Nepal, fostered by ancient Hindu and Buddhist culture, are of an astonishing richness, especially in the valley of Kathmandu. The tri-city of Nepal, Kathmandu, Patan and Bhadgaon are very rich in religious shrines, art and architecture. These cities are described as the open air museums. These cities contain many religious temple, stupas, monasteries and historical monuments. There are many other places of pilgrimage outside Kathmandu valley. Just to mention Lumbini—the nativity of Gautam Buddha, the prince of peace, Janakpur the birth place of Sita—daughter of the King Janak and consort of Rama hero of great Hindu epic Ramayana, many other temples, stupas, Gompas and places of pilgrimage scattered all over the country.

PLACES OF PILGRIMAGE

Nepal possesses important shrines of Buddhism and Hinduism which are visited annually by great number of pilgrims from Nepal and abroad. Innumerable pilgrims visit the stupa of Swayambhunath, Pashupatinath and other important shrines during the big festival each year. There are many religious sites in Kathmandu valley which are big attractions for international tourism. The people of Nepal are extremely religious and observe traditional customs and rites. Nepal is the only country in the world and has a tradition of religious tolerance which is truely amazing.

There are many places of pilgrimage in Nepal and there is now every step is being taken to develop pilgrimage outside the Kathmandu valley. His Majesty Government has taken every possible priority to foster pilgrimage tourism to the shrines of Bharachetra, Janakpur, Gosainkunda, Muktinath and Dhanusha.

Lumbini, the birth-place of Gautama Buddha holds the greatest international significance and it is one of the four major poles of Buddhist pilgrimage. Lumbini, being the sacred place for the Buddhist which is sure to play a major role in future pilgrimage and tourism.

PLACES OF PILGRIMAGES INSIDE KATHMANDU VALLEY

Pashupatinath—Lord Pashupatinath is the guardian deity of Nepal. One of the sacred Hindu temples dedicated to Lord Shiva is situated some 5 kilometres from Kathmandu city and on the banks of the Bagmati river. The golden temple of Pashupatinath is a double-roofed pagoda of gold-gilted. The gateways are plated with pure silver. This temple abodes the lingam of Pashupatinath. This holy place is a jumble of innumerable temples and shrines dominated by the colossal image of Nandi (Bull) the mount of Shiva. There is a crematorium outside the temple by the side of the river, Bagmati. On the annual festival of Shivaratri (February/March) many pilgrims not only from all parts of Nepal but also from India visit to pay homage to Shiva.

Boudhnath—This is one of the world's largest and oldest Buddhist stupa, lying eight kilometers east of Kathmandu. The shrine is a hemisphere on a four-stage plinth. It is built on a octagonal base. It has about eighty small recesses each hearing the image of the Buddha. The four sides are decorated with the grave and mystic eyes of Lord Buddha.

Swayambhunath—This most glorious Buddhist stupa is considered to be a 2000 years old. It is located three kilometres west of Kathmandu city on a hillock The stupa is a large hemisphere representing the Garbha which signifies the womb, the seat of creation. It is surrounded by a gold gilt square projection which in turn is crowned by the Chudamani, a conical canopy of gilt rings. From each of the four sides of the space a pair of unwinking eyes—all seeing eyes of Adi Buddha are engraved. There are other several miniature stupas and shrines around the stupa including a pagoda temple of Harati, the Hindu Goddess of epidemics. It shows the religious feature of the Nepali culture—Hindu and Buddhist religion forming unity.

Budanilkantha—This holy place has an ancient image of reclining Lord Vishnu on the beds of snakes at the base of Shivapuri hill. It is located about eight kilometers north of Kathmandu. It is also a very famous place of pilgrimage for Hindus.

Dakshinkali—Lying at a scenic spot some 25 km. south-west of Kathmandu, is dedicated to Goddess Kali, important places of pilgrimage of Hindus to offer their prayers.

Changu Narayan—This is also an ancient temple of God Vishnu, on a hilltop 13 kilometres east of Kathmandu.

This is believed to be the oldest pagoda temple of the valley, artistic heritage of the Lichhavian era. It is an ancient historical place situated on a hillock named Kileswara and there is a composite image representing Lokeshawra upon Vishnu, Garud and a lion. This temple was built by Vishnu. Gupta and later renovated by Hari Dutta. The temple is richly decorated with sculptures and carvings. The courtyard of this temple has the inscriptions on stone pillars, wood and copper which gives the ancient glory of Nepal.

PLACES OF PILGRIMAGE IN DIFFERENT PARTS OF THE COUNTRY

Gorkha—The old kingdom of the present Shah dynasty is a beautiful natural hill region with the Gorkha Durbar and the temples of Gorakhnath and Kali atop the hill. The famous pilgrimage spot Manakamana lies south-east from Gorkha.

Manakamana—This is also the famous pilgrimage spot of Nepal. It is very near from Gorkha. Every Nepali is very ambitious to make a pilgrim trip to Manakamana. It lies south-east from Gorkha Cable Car to this sacred place is started from the Kurin (Cheres) Chitwan and takes 8 minutes to reach.

Swarga Dwari—This holy place is situated 26 kilometres west of Khalanga Bazar administrative headquarters of Puthan district. It signifies the meaning (the Gate of Heavens). It is one of the country's most venerated Hindu pilgrimage spots. Sage Padma Giri, famed as Swarga Dwari Mahaprabhu made Swarga Dwari famous. It is located at an altitude of 2,122 m. full of scenic panorama of the Himalaya.

Janakpur—Janakpur is the ancient city of Janak, the wise king of Mithila. Janakpur is stated on the south-east of Kathmandu. This place is famous for its marble temple of Janaki. Janakpur is an epic famed town and birth-place of Sita, consort of Rama, the hero of epic Ramayana. It is another site of pilgrimage situated in the district of Mahottari in Nepal. It is a beautiful and historic city dating back to ancient time. Legend epitomises it that Sita, heroine of the Hindu epic Ramayana was born here and later got married with the legendary Rama is the same city. The city's most famous landmark is the large and artistic marble temple of Janaki built by Queen Vrisha Bhanu of the Indian state of Tikamgarh. Close to it, other ancient shrine known as Rama temple. Besides, these two temples, there are sacred waterpools. During the festival of Ram Nawami and Bibaha Panchami, thousand of Hindu pilgrims from India and from various parts of Nepal assemble here to offer homage to Lord Rama and her consort Sita. The marble temple is famous for its intricately decorated cupolas, ceilings and tiles in the Indo-Persia style. Janakpur is linked by air from Kathmandu. Accommodations are available. Sita Bibaha festival (November-December) a lovely procession moves from the temple of Rama, taking the image dressed as a bridegroom to the Janaki temple.

Dhanusha—This religious site is located about twenty kilometers not-east of Janakpur. This legend has said that Rama, the hero of Ramayana epic, had broken the great Shiva

Dhanu (the great Bow of God Shiva) into various pieces which had scattered on this place. Due to this occurrence, the site derived it name Dhanusha from the Great Dhanu or Bow. Many devotees visit this place every Sunday on the month of Magh, take a ritual bath in the holy water and pay homage to this place. During the Ram Navami and Bibaha Panchami festivals, melas (fairs) are took place at Dhanusha. It is significant as a religious centre of Hindu pilgrimage because it is the place where Rama showed talent of extra-ordinary feats by breaking bow into pieces and got Sita in a marriage.

The Shrines of Bharachetra—This is the most important religious site in eastern Nepal. It is situated at the confluence of the Koka and Koshi rivers. This place is known for its two Varaha images (the idol of God Boar-incarnation of God Vishnu). This place is reknown as a pilgrimage site since the sixth to the seventh centuries A.D. This is a place sacred to Hinduism and pole for national and international Hindu pilgrims. This is one of Nepal's prominent places of pilgrimage and can be found mentioned in the Hindu scripture.

Gosainkunda—This is one of the famous pilgrimage site in Nepal. It is famous for its religious lake of Gosainkunda located at an altitude of 5,100 meters above sea level. It is located to the north-east of Kathmandu and a venerated place of pilgrimage. It is 132 kilometres. This is a sacred place of Hindu pilgrimage. The proper route to visit from Kathmandu to Gosainkinda is through Dhunche. Gosainkunda lake is surrounded by higher mountain towards the east and west and commands picturesque sight. There are nine other equally famous lakes on the east and west of the main Gosainkunda lake. Many pilgrims visit this pilgrimage spot during the festivals of Dashain and Janai Purnima and take holy dip is the lake and take part in the grand fair organised in the celebration of this occasion. This place requires fifteen to twenty days to traverse. This place is famous for beautiful landscapes, glacial lakes, waterfalls and evergreen forests. This is one of the famous pilgrimage of Nepal and thousands of people trek annually in the month of August on a pilgrimage to the glacial lake. This lake is considered to be the abode of God Shiva.

Muktinath—The reknown temple of God Muktinath is situated in the district of Mustang and is 3749 m on a high mountain ridge. It is about 18 kilometres north-east of Jomson. While going to the holy place of Muktinath, the trail starts from the picturesque valley of Pokhara. All along the trail from Pokhara to Jomsom, the natural panorama is very impressive. The whole area opens out in all its serenity, grandeur and colour, set amidst all splendours of snow-capped peaks of Machhapuchare, Annapurna, Daulagiri, Nilgiri etc. The landscape is arid and rocky from Jomsom with patches of green cultivation.

Muktinath is equally visited both by Hindu and Buddhist pilgrims. It is a revered pilgrimage spot nestled in the arid Himalayan Canyons. The Holy site of Muktinath is said to have the terminus of earth, air, fire and water and these four elements are the source from where power generates. There is a pagoda temple of Jwala Mai equally worshipped both by the Hindus and the Buddhists alike. Surrounding the temple a stone wall encircles one hundred and eight full head shaped brass water spouts. This place abounds in sacred Saligrams along the Kali Gandaki river beds containing fossilized ammonites. The Jwala Mai—a hot natural flame comes out of rock as a miraculous fire. This black stone is sacred to Hindus and is considered emblems of Vishnu Narayan. It takes almost a forthright to reach this route from Pokhara. The routes are full of lovely mountains, dazzling springs, splashing waterfalls coming down with torrential splashes and revulets passing through Verdant Valleys. The shrine of Muktinath is venerated and worshipped by Tibetans as well and they have constructed some of Gompas or monasteries near to the shrine.

There are many natural passes for communicating between Tibet and Nepal. Some of these passes as Kuti Pass Mustang Pass, Hatia Pass, Rakha La Pass etc. are well known sence ancient time. The tibetans usually visit into Nepal along these passes for trade of salt and other goods.

Damodar Kund—This is also a famous Himalayan pilgrimage place in the west of Muktinath. There is a big lake in the midst of snow-covered mountains all along its sides.

Lumbini—The birth-place of Lord Buddha is situated on the western Terai of Nepal. Lost to the world for a millennium, without any traces, the site of Gautama Buddha's birth-place was rediscovered by archaeologists at the time of the present century, place for the Buddhist and a sacred pilgrimage site. It is south of the first foothills of the Himalayas, the Churia range.

Lumbini lies is a very ancient place called Rupandehi district in the Lumbini zone of Nepal. Gautama Buddha was born in Lumbini Park in 623 B.C. under a Sal grove (Sorea robusta) on the full moon day of the sixth month of the lunar calender. He was born on the full moon day of Baishak Purnima and this day is the most important and unique day for the Buddhist. His birth, enlightenment and emancipation (nirvana) were also on Baishak Purnima. This Baishak Purnima is also popular by the name of Buddha Purnima among the Buddhist in Nepal and all over the world.

Lumbini has been accounted, along with Bodh Gaya, Sarnath and Kushinagar in India (the places of His enlightenment, first Serman and emancipation (nirvana) respectively as one of the four sacred places of pilgrimage. So it rises to an equal standing with the holy places dedicated to other world religions. Gautama Buddha proclaimed the glorious doctrine for the gain of the many, for the welfare of the many and in compassion for the world.

His Majesty Government of Nepal requested technical assistance from the United Nations in 1967. In 1967 the late United Nations Secretary general U-Thant visited the sacred Garden Lumbini. A Mission sent by the United Nations Development Programme (UNDP) and the United Nations Educational Scientific and Cultural Organisations (UNESCO) came for making studies and evaluations of the requirement for the development of the area. As recommended by the UNDP consultant Mission, the Master Plan for the Lumbini prepared by Messrs Kenzo Tange and URTEC world famous architect of Japan has now implemented phase-wise. In 1970, the thirteen National International Lumbini Development Committee was formed in New York. Lumbini Development

Trust (LTD) is created in 198 under Lumbini Development Trust Act 2042.

The old monastery the artistic stone image of Maya Devi is proved by the historians that the existance of this image from the twelfth century. Many projects involved such aspects—road construction airport expansion, water supply electrification, communication, land acquisition, landscaping and flood control are going on and many of them are finally completed. International participation is very enthusiastic and Lumbini is now no more a remote place in the south-west part of Nepal due to a major restoration and development works. The visitor has now facilities for stay and foodings. There is road to visit these from the Siddhartha Nagar (Bhairahawa) known as Lumbini Highway just in a half hour drive. Bhairahawa airport is nearly 150 kilometres north-east of Kathmandu and forty-five minute plane flight from Kathmandu. Hokke club of Japan has constructed a four star hotel there for the comfort of pilgrims. Now landscaping has given the same beauty as it was at the time of Buddha's mother Maya Devi. Lumbini, after the full implementation of the development plans would acquire major significance as a place of pilgrimage and tourist attraction. It is a Gem of cultural and historical importance to international visitors. Nepal, the land sanctified by the birth of Lord Buddha, has eternal, charm. Lumbini is sure to provide repose and rest for the teaming Buddhist millions from all over the world enjoying spiritual and unusual message of peace and compassion propounded by Gautama Buddha, the prince of peace. Lumbini is included in the World Heritage list by the World Heritage Committee on December 9, 1997.

Lumbini attracs Buddhist pilgrims from all over the world. Lumbini, the birth place of Buddha is one of the world's great centres of the Buddhist faith.

FESTIVALS

Nepal's festival has an audio-visual impact of unforgettable dimension. It is followed by a wide variety of songs dances and music. It also focuses a rare costume parade.

Nepal is the land of festivals. Festivals are not merely spectacle for the Nepali people but they are part of the glorious cultural heritage. Festivals find together the Nepalese people of diverse cultural backgrounds and beliefs into one nation. Different faiths practised in Nepal is manifested in the numerous festivals of Nepal. There are colourful and appealing festivals practically every fortnight. Whether of local or national character, the festival is associated sacred either to Hindu or Buddhist mythology and people celebrate it as common to all in the same spirit of solemnity and happily. Nepal is unique among the countries the world in having such close understanding among the Hindus and Buddhists resulting in a cultural synthesis not noticed anywhere else. Apart from the religious significance festivals may be linked with the remembrance of dead family members, to herald the coming of different seasons, to mark the beginning or end of the agricultural cycle, or just family celebrations.

On the festival occasion, the Nepali people take their ritual holy bath in a river or lake, worship their deities, visit temples, stupas or shrines and undertake feasting as well as ritual fasting.

Most spectacular festivals are undoubtedly those in Kathmandu Valley. The valley of Kathmandu has images of many Hindu and Buddhist divinities enshrined in their various temples and shrines. The festivals are primarily connected with one of the Gods and Goddesses of both the religion and form a colourful spectacle of human verve and joy among the all people of Nepal.

Anyone who visits here from the later part of August through October is sure to be surprised by the constant succession of festival taking place. As soon as Gayjatra, the festival of cows draws to a close, there follows God Krishna's birthday, the Teej, a festival solely for women and the Indra Jatra Festival, closely linked to the Kumari, the living Goddesses of Kathmandu. These are soon followed by the Grandest of all Nepal's festivals, Dasara with all sorts of masked dances. In the high lands, these are many spectacular festivals like Mani Rimbu which are famous for marked dances.

The religious festivals are just common as the carved decorations with some sources claiming that a festival is being held somewhere in the land in the order of once every three days. In some festivals, shamanistic rituals are also practiced and faith healers and witch-doctors can be seen in their peculiar attires and drums do away devils and spirits.

Different festivals and popular religious fairs and melas take place through out the year. Religious festivals bring life and colour around all temples and stupas. Some festivals are really impressive and fantastic with people's maifestations with their triumphat chariots made of big structures with massive painted wheels pulled by them with joy and excitement. The happy crowd of young people and their joyful bands with trumpets, cymbals, drums, the girl with colourful costumes of the procession following them contribute to make Nepal a paradise for the music recorder and for the photographer.

Nepali people's passion for rhythm finds creature expression through a wide range of festivals which have been evolved over the countries. Festivals are frequent in Nepal and invariably attained by performances of the classical masked dance which are a popular feature of the country's social and religious life. The classical dance is based on themes taken from the rich and elaborate mythology of the Hindu and Buddhist religion. Such dancers are performed in open quadragle or a roused platform as part of the yearly celebration of some festival or the other in Kathmandu, Patan and Bhadgaon. There are various types of musical instruments. All these melodic and tonal instruments are played as part of any big festival. They set mood of the festival and a sonic backdrop to it. Festivals are celebrated by a wide variety of songs, dances and music.

Festival Calender

Some of the important festivals are listed below. Since most festival dates depend on the stuffing lunar calender, exact dates can not be forcasted but only the month in which they occur can be given.

December-January—National Unification Day—This is celebrated as a unification day and the birth-anniversary of the late King Prithvi Narayan Shah the Great, the Founder of modern Nepal throughout Nepal. A very colourful ceremony is held in front of the Singha Durbar Gate, Kathmandu. (Public Holiday)

December—The official birthday of His Majesty King Birendra Bir Bickram Shah Dev, the present monarch. This event is observed by the illumination of public buildings, bonfires, parades and processions. (Public Holiday)

January-February—Maghe Sankranti—This occasion marks the turning point from water solstice to the summer solstice. Big fairs are held at Dhunge Sangu in Pokhara and Narayan Ghat in Bharatpur where many people gather to take sacred baths.

February-March—Sri Panchami—First day of commencement of spring, family and village celebrations. It is also a festival of Saraswati, Goddess of Learning. (Government Holiday)

February-March—National Democratic Day—It is observed as a commemoration day of democracy. Procession and other celebrations occur all over the country. (National Holiday)

February-March—Maha Shiva Ratri—Nepal's most celebrated festival which draws throng of pilgrims from far and wide. It is observed in all Shiva Temple as the night of Lord Shiva. Hindu devotees from all over India and Nepal who visit to pay homage to Lord Shiva at Pashupatinath Temple situated in Kathmandu. (Government Holiday)

August—Janai Purnima—A festival in which Hindus wearing sacred threads take a ritualistic bath and take yellow bands in their wraist with Brahmin priests.

August—Gaijatra—This gay carnival type of festival is

celebrated impressively in Kathmandu, Patan, Bhadgaon, Pokhara, Tansen and Dankuta. It is performed in memory of dead Members of the family by sending cows or persons wearing cow-like decorations in a procession. Many hilarious figures and comic episodes are carried in a procession.

August—Matayaa—A local Buddhist festival of Patan. A crowd of devotees playing music and dancing go round all the chaityas of the city from early morning till late afternoon.

August-September—Krishnastami—This is observed to make the birth-day of Lord Krishna, one of the incarnation of Vishnu and epic of hero of Mahabharata. There is an impressive ceremony of the Krishna temple in Patan and Changu Narain.

September—Teej—This is the festival solely for women. Hindu women hold a complete fast, visit temples of Shiva and his consort. It is most colourful to see at Pasupatinath temple in Kathmandu and Ramghat in Pokhara.

September—Indra Jatra—This is the most illustrative festival held in Kathmandu. This festival is celebrated for a whole week and is celebrated by playing of music, marked dances and feasts in praise of the God Indra, the God of rain. The chariot festival of living Goddess of Kathmandu is also observed by putting her in a chariot and drawing it all through the traditional routes of the old city of Kathmandu. This is the most dramatic festival of Kathmandu.

September-October—Bada Dasai or Durga Puja—This is the national festival of Nepal. It is celebrated for ten days. A procession of government officials carry Phulpati (leaves and flowers brought mainly for this occasion all way from Gorkha) sacrifices of goats are made at Kot Hanuman Dhoka in Kathmandu. Khadgajatra, the sword festival is held Tebahal and other localities of Kathmandu. A traditional mask dance is held at Patan Durbar Square. This festival is observed as the victory of good over evil and the victory of Rama, hero of Hindu epic Ramayana over the demon Ravana.

November-December—Balachaturdasi—This festival is held

in honour of dead ancestors. It is most colourful to see at Pashupatinath in Kathmandu on the preceding night of this festival. People congregate by singing songs and lighting lamps at night.

October-December—Tihar-Lakshmipuja—This is the festival of lights people worship Lakshmi—the Goddess of wealth. This festival is observed for five days—First day as the day of crow, second day is the day of dogs, third day is the day of cow, fifth day is day of the Bull and fifth day as brothers day are worshipped. Brothers and sisters present gifts.

December—Vivaha Panchami—This is a grand festival of Janakpur in Dhanusa district in eastern Terai. This occasion commemorates the marriage of Sita to Rama. One of the most venerated Hindu festival.

February—Loshar—This festival is most impressively observed by all the Tibetan speaking populations including the Sherpas. Dances in Khumbu, Helambu and other northern regions of Nepal are impressive.

March-April—Holi or Fagu—It is festival of colour and throwing of coloured powers. A long pole is erected at Basantpur Hanuman Dhoka, ancient place complex, Kathmandu as a start of this festival with strips of colourful cloth. (Public Holiday).

March-April—Ghodejatra—This festival is associated with a demon Guru Mapa. Processions and horse-racing take place. The Royal Nepalese Army organises a horse race in Tundikhel in Kathmandu. A public festival takes place in which certain divinities are brought in chariots in the day time in Assan, a locality in the old town of Kathmandu and in the evening to Tundikhel. It is a festival of both religious and secular.

March-April—A chariot Festival of white Machhendranath. This festival in honour of the white Machhendranath of Kel Tole in Kathmandu. A big Chariot carrying the divinity is drawn through the streets of Kathmandu for several days.

April—Ram Nawami—This day celebrates the birth of Rama. One of the incarnation of Vishnu a prominent Hindu God.

April—Matatertha Aunsi or Mother day—Mothers are presented with sweets and gifts by their sons and daughters. For those who are motherless make ritual offerings to the departed mothers (Government Holiday).

April—A Chariot Festival of Red Machchendranath. An image of Machchendra, a deity mainly known as the God of rain, is installed on a massive four-wheeled chariot and pulled through the streets in Patan by hundreds of devotees.

April—Nava Barsha—Nepal's new year day in accordance with lunar calender. At Bhadgaon, the Bisket festival is celebrated on this day. At Span Tertha and Bagdwar in the outskirts of Kathmandu, people go to take bath. A feature of this festival Bisket is the raising of a tall, decorated mast, festival with long strips of material some 60 feet high. A number of colourful procession and ceremonies take place in connection with the festival as the day which precede it.

April-May—Buddha Jayanti—Full moon day of May—Celebration of birth, enlightment and death of the Gautam Buddha. This festival marks the birthday of Gautama, the Buddha, founder of Buddhism and a great son of Nepal. The nativity of Gautama Buddha, Lumbini is in Nepal. It is observed through worship in all the Buddhist shrines of Nepal, especially at Lumbini, his birth place and at Swayambhunath and Bodhnath in Kathmandu.

July—Dumji—This festival is celebrated by the Sherpas.

Nepal has the cultural heritage as she has the combination of elements to attract the attention of tourists and provoke a visit by them. This combination represents the supply of Nepal Tourist Market. Nepal has its source in a temple, stupa, a monuments, unique landscape, lofty Himalayan peaks, living species of animals and vegetations or a piece of handicrafts active handicraft (bronze, wood and brass) in Patan, pottery in Thimi, wood carving and painting in Patan and Bhaktapur, carpet making in Patan, pashmina wool materials in Jumla, Syangbochhe and other places testify that the traditional art is still living.

The place of pilgrimage and cultural tourism in Nepal is very great. "Among the Mountains, I am the Himalaya"—Lord Krishna in Bhagvad Gita testifies about the sanctity of Nepal as one of the holiest place on earth. The Himalaya, or the 'Abode of Snow' is referred to as the early home of Lord Shiva and his consort, Parvati. The Himalaya has a particular importance to the follower of Hinduism since time immemorial. The Mythological period covering the Satya, Treta and Dwapar yugas or ages also contains numerous references regarding the temples, shrines and holy places of the country. Many reflections are expressed in the ancient Hindu and Buddhists texts about the holiness of Nepal as the land of spiritual blessing and tranquility.

The book containing the rules of language describes Nepal as "Ne Munina Palitam Nepalam" the land protected by sage Ne is Nepal. Many sages and seers preferred the serene environ and quiet natural atmosphere of Nepal as the best place for their meditation. To the Hindus, it is the holy land of Lord Pashupatinath. Many philosopher—saints like Viswamitra, Kapila, Yajnavalka, Balmiki and Raja Janak found endless spiritual inspiration while penancing by the sacred banks of the Kosh, Gandaki and Karnali rivers or in the pristine Sagarmatha (Mount Everest) Daulagiri and Annapura mountain. Their in-depth observations and analyses of concrete phenomena regarding Hindu religiosity still dominate the intellectual area. All these great thinkers attained perfection in their spirituality here. The hermitage of all of them was in the tranquil recesses of Nepal.

Nepal, the birth place of Sakya Muni Buddha, is one of the world's great centres of the Buddhist faith. Buddhism has its origin in the teaching of Sakya Muni Buddha, who was born in the southern Terai of Nepal circa 563 B.C. Buddhist shrines and sites combine to represent it as the holy places for teeming millions of Buddhists from all over the world.

Religiously rich, Nepal is the meeting ground of the great civilizations of Asia and as such she is the cultural museum where religious shrines art treasures and monuments of historical interest are preserved.

In view of a vast and rich natural and cultural heritage of Nepal, significant goals in tourism development should be to place emphasis on the preservation and protection of some areas and to improve the quality of the historical, recreational and other tourist attractions and accommodations, rather than on intensive campaigns to increase the quantity of tourism activity in the country. Such an approach provides ultimate social as well as economic benefits to the country.

5

ADVENTURE AND SPORT TOURISM

Nepal is a land unique in many ways. Despite the small size of the country, it has an astonishing diversity of cultures and natural attractions. Nepal's varigated picturesque panorama and its mystical charm has been attracting people since it opened its door for international visitors.

The different topography of the country provides it with a wide variety of climatic conditions, varying from the freezing cold of the Himalayan zone to the warm heat of the Terai, the midland hills and green valleys between them have a soothing climate.

Nepal is a source of perennial love for the inquisitive, bold and adventures. So many visitors who have travelled, narrated it as a destination of many different ethnic people with hospitable traits, many animals, birds, flowers, many cultural activities, with distinct customs and traditions, collection of magnificent arts and architecture, unspolit nature beauties and attractions. Being situated in the Trans-Asian route, it is a destination of a unique and charming trourism potentials characteristic of its own, quite different from other tourist destinations of the world.

Nepal is among the most fascinating regions of the world for adventurers. It is magnificent country with ancient culture with a rich and beautiful heritage. Side by side with it, the natural landscape is majestic. The towering Himalayas stand awesome and majestic with their snow capped peaks posing an open challenge to adventurers, mountaineers and explorers from around the world. Nepal Himalaya includes many major peaks of the world. Sagarmatha (Mount Everest), Kanchanjunga, Lhotse, Makalu, Dhaulgiri, Mansalu, Cho-oyu and Annapurna-all having eight thousands meters height. These Himalayan peaks and their towering miracles of nature are always becoming the challenge to the mountaineers of the world.

The temperature, climate and rainfall of Nepal differ from place to place. Terai, the southern region has a tropical hot climate all the year. The central mountain region has a subtropical cool climate. The northern Himalayan region has an alpine climate. The Terai region is famous for many national parks and wild life reserves which are famous for viewing many rare animals and birds.

There is no dearth of things to do in Nepal for the adventurer or energetic. This is long trek or jungle safari and white-water rafting. To more ardeous and adventures, there is mountain climbing of various heights and dimensions. The relaxed visitor can confine nature and culture with mountain viewing from a variety of look-out points and historical towns throughout Nepal.

Adventure tourism has a big potential for Nepal due to remoteness and inaccessibility apart from the inhospitable and often forbidding nature. These characteristic have preserved large areas of unique wilderness in Nepal which provides a potential for recreational use.

Adventure tourism can be enjoyed in Nepal due to inherent potential it holds. The anticipated trend towards activity oriented vacation, mountation recreation in the Himalayas can provide an alternative form of this type of holiday which is today entirely focused on seaside recreation. A Nepal adventure holiday is able to offer everything that is indeterminate group expects of a sporting, recreative and cultural holiday. There is choice of adventure which consist of trekking in the mountain terrain for a week or even for a month by trekking up to the Everest base camp. For the more adventurous visitor, there is white-water rafting in the fast flowing rivers of the glacial waters of the various rivers of Nepal. The nature lover can arrange safari tour to the Terai on the elephant back to observe stampeding rhinos and stalking tigers. There are plenty of opportunities for glidding, hot-water balooning, mountain bycycling and mountain marathoning in the splendid natural surroundings. Viewing spotted deer or variety of birds, comforting wild animals while on forest excursion, canoeing or swimming in the blue lakes or in the snow-fed waters of a Himalayan rivers, trekking through the villages and mountain terrains—these are the activities which can be taken by adventurer or energetic visitor. There is no denying the fact that Nepal has great adventure potential in the region—few countries can offer such a big contrast of natural beauty.

Nepal Himalaya is the challenge for adventures. They offer tremendous sceneries with the enduring charm for alpinists, explorers, mountaineers and adventurers. The central portion of the great mountain mass which traverses through Nepal is the most dignified and rugged. Here is Majestic splendour, Mount Everest, scaled and climbed many times but awesome and unchallenged, fans out with spectacular Kanchanjunga, Makalu, Dhaulagiri, Lhotse, Nuptse, Ama Dablam and Annapurna all, in their supreme beauty among mountains. Physically, this mountain mass is lord of all, vast in unchallenged and isolaged supremacy which the mountaineers of the world look to reach their summits and to explore nature's stronghold annually applying for permission to climbing.

Nepal dreams and adventure travel supervised holiday with excitement and novelty but relaxed enough to enable a visitor the magnificent scenery, rare wildlife, culture and religions of this fascinating part of Asia. Nepal Himalaya and various natural panorama provide an opportunity to live adventurer's dreams.

MOUNTAINEERING

Nepal Himalaya or "the Abode of the Snow" is the youngest and highest mountain system of the world. This mountain system was evolved by a collison between two tectonic plates 50 millions years ago. It dominates over 2,400 kilometers as a colossal south-facing range between the Indus Brahmaputra rivers with Nanga Parbat (8125 m) and Namcha Barwa (7755 m) as its terminal high points. Eight hundred kilometers of its central section traverses through Nepal and is known as Nepal Himalaya. Here congregate more than 250 peaks that exceed 6,000 meters in height a unique concentration of lofty dazzling summits. Out of the 31 Himalayan peaks over 7,600 meters, 22 are in Nepal Himalaya including eight of the world's fourteen highest giants.

Nepal's physical location and character is regarded as unique and spectacular. The major part of the country is of high mountains and rolling hills. It accounts for about 83 percent of the total land area and the remaining 17 percent is occupied by the flat lands of the Terai. The altitude varies from 152 m above sea level in the Terai in the south to more than 8848 m in the Northern Himalayas. Though only 145 kilometers in width, Nepal displays a singular variety of geographical regions ranging from the tropical lowlands to the arctic plateau. This extreme variation of topography and flora is matched by Nepal's rich cultural and ethic diversity. Nature has endured Nepal with a spectacular phenomena and vast treasures of attractions are now for visitors to enjoy.

Nepal Himalaya represent one of the majestic features of the Nepalese landscape. Eight of the world's fourteen peaks exceeding 8,000 m are in Nepal. Sagarmatha (Mount Everest), the highest peak in the world (8848 m) is 156 kilometers east of Kathmandu. English climber George Leigh Mallory upon first seeing Everest known to Tibetans as Chomolungma, or "Goddess mother of the world" and to Nepali as Sagarmatha "sky head" wrote "lord of all vast in unchallenged and isolated supremacy". Nepal Himalaya is really supreme, awesome majestic and mysterious. Standing as sentinels all across the northern border of Nepal, whether it is to Everest, Makalu, Annapurna, Dhaulgiri, Lhotse, Mansalu or Kanchanjunga all are becoming the inspirations and desires of the mountaineers of the world to climb their tops. The mountaineers are tempted to scale these mountains as French mountaineer Loinel Terray calls it the "Conquest of the useless". Similarly, George Leigh Mallory said in a characteristic British tone "Because it's there." Whatever the reasons, each year many mountaineers of different nations of the world apply for permission to climb Nepal Himalaya, taking up the challenge of formidable hardships.

Nepal Himalaya is a stunning blend of snow-capped peaks, mighty cloffs, massive glaciers, a drifting ravines and deep gorges. Beneath its shadow lies the lush green valleys covered by green mountains and meadows and further down again exist fertile valleys. The valleys are full of lovely villages full of pine and rhododendron groves and traversed by snowfed rivers. The inner Himalaya consists of labyrinth of ranges some fifty miles in depth descending between the Great Himalayas and the Churia Hills adjoining the bordering Terai, The Mahabharat Lekh—a typical well-defined range of mountains expanding from the Mahakali to beyond the Kosi valley. The ridges of mountains of the Mahabharat range present a steep slope towards the south and a relatively smooth beside towards the north. The northern and north-eastern slopes are covered by dense forest followed higher up by a snow. The southern slopes except in the protected valleys are nacked, to steep to maintain a soil covering for the growth of vegetations. To the north of the Mahabharat range lies the Kathmandu valley. another mountain region is the churia Hills along the southern border of Nepal, the Churia Hills, geologically or succession of the Siwalik range rise gently from the plains within the region, there is a escarpments of narrow ridges, separated by more or less wide valleys enclosing northwest southwest parts of it. These valleys called as "Duns" are a dominent feature of the foothills of Nepal. Southward is situated the steep slope known as Bhabar. South of the Bhabar and the Churia Hills is the Terai-lowland of alluvial plains.

Within the short sketch of 150 miles which separates her southern border from those of the north, Nepal soars steeply to the breadth-taking Himalayan snowy peaks.

Nepal Himalaya is the loftiest mountain ranges in the world and covers the world's highest and also the most majestic summits. Towards the west, Nepal extends beyond the Himalayan range to the Trans-Himalayan area which is like the barren Tibetan plateau, being a part of Tibetan topography. This spectacular complex and unique topography forms the singular attraction of Nepal.

MOUNTAINEERING : THE CHALLENGE FOR ADVENTURISTS

The Himalayas cast one of the dignified features of the Nepalese landscapes. They signify "the abode of snow" shinning blend of snow and ice. Nepal has already well-established with her snowy and challenging peaks. It has the greatest concentration of High Himalayas with so many peaks still to be climbed and glaciers to be explored. These are said to be over 1310 peaks above 6000 meters throughout the country. They include eight out of 14 highest peaks of the world above 8000 meters. This is the reason, Nepal has become a focal point for mountaineering from all over the world and as a centre of mountaineering activities.

The magnificent mountain mass of Nepal Himalaya is a lure for world mountaineers. Her mountains have been the dream and goal of explorers, scientists and mountaineers. The stories of the climbers for great summits for Nepal Himalaya have made Nepal so popular among the people of the world that there is great desire among all sectors of international visitors to have a glimpse of the Nepal Himalayas and at least to be near or to climb the summit. The number of expedition teams to climb various Nepal Himalayan peaks has constantly been increasing for the last ten years. Nepal Himalayan can be divided into three categories as follows:

Above eight thousand meters Eight thousanders	Eight of the fourteen highest peaks in the world.
Above seven thousand meters Seven Thousanders	One hundred twenty seven peaks.
Above six thousand meters Six Thousanders	One thousand one hundred sixty six peaks.

Mountaineering can be called sporting tourism. It is very much popular among the mountaineers of the world. All Nepal Himalaya having the height of six thousand meters to eight thousand eight hundred forty eight meters are applied annually for climbing. So it can be said that major aspect of the tourism in Nepal is the snow-clad mountains with its unique natural beauty regarded as earth's most spectacular tourist attractions. The colossal mountain mass of Nepal Himalaya is a attraction not for world's mountaineers but also represents a fundamental asset to recreational use and an important facet for tourism.

The first decade of mountaineering was started in 1949. Surveying and reconnaissance were leading activities of the initial period from the later half of the 19th century to 1949. The first decade of mountaineering was 1949-1960 and Nepal allowed mountaineering expedition to climb its mountains. The pioneering exploration and mountaineering expedition teams in 1949 were one British team in the Langtang-Ganesh Himal region and a Swiss team in the Kanchanjunga area. By the end of first decade (1949-1960) total number of eighty four large and small expedition had participated in climbing activities in the Nepal Himalaya. Some fourteen nations participated in the first decade comprised of large and small expeditions. The British participated with 27 expeditions, the Japanese with seventeen expeditions, the Swiss ten, the French six, Austria three, and Newzealand two expeditions. Other nations such as India, USA, Argentina, Australia, Canada, Denmark and West Germany also applied for mountaineering expeditions. The first decade was a decade of pioneer mountaineering which combined reconnaissance and climbing. But the outcome of the expeditions were impressive. All the Eight Thousands of the Nepal Himalaya were scaled and climbed as for example

Annapurna in 1950, Sagarmatha (Mount Everest) in 1953, Cho oyu in 1954, Kanchanjunga and Makalu in 1955, Lho Tse and Manaslu in 1956 Dhaulagiri in 1960. The episode of expedition to Sagarmatha (Mount Everest) the highest peak in the world was highlighted in 1953 with the successful expedition for the first time by Tenzing Sherpa and Edmund Hillary on the coronation day of Queen Ellegabeth II.

The second decade of Nepal mountaineering (1961-1970) was highlighted by the participation of one hundred five expedition teams from seventeen countries. Japan took part with the largest number of 48 expedition teams. United Kingdom participated with 15 expeditions, W. Germany 8, India six, and the Netherlands and Austraila had four each. U.S.A. and Australia sent three expedition teams. Newzealand, France, Switzerland, Italy and Yugoslavia sent two each. Czechoslovakia, Denmark and Spain participated with one expedition each, two were international expeditions. The first ascents included Ama Dablan, Annapurna III, Nuptse, Chamlang, Jaunu, Nilgiri, North Pumori, Kangtega, Number, Saipal, Glacier Dome, Gangapurna, Rock Noir, Gyachang Kang, Annapurna South, Boudha, Churia Himal Peak 29 and Lho Tse Shar. Mountaineering was banned for during 1965-68 in Nepal due to political reasons.

The third decade of Mountaineering in the Nepal Himalaya (1971-81) witnessed an unprecedented increase in foreign expeditions. It reached 404 figures of mountaineering expeditons by different countries as against 105 in the second decade. The administration of mountaineering expeditions was handled by the section of Ministry of Foreign Affairs of His Majesty's Government of Nepal before 1977. But in view of increasing number of mountaineering expeditions and to manage mountain tourism in Nepal more systematically and scientifically, His Majesty's Government of Nepal, constituted the Ministry of Tourism in 1977 with a section to look after mountaineering expeditions. Ministry of Tourism, promulgated tourism Act 1978 and mountaineering expedition regulations in 1979 after careful planning and research for the smooth development of mountaineering in Nepal.

Due to an increase in the number of mountaineering expedition teams, His Majesty's Government of Nepal rationalised mountaineering management with the recognition of multiple routes to undivided peaks and extension of climbing season.

The year 1981 witnessed 74 expedition teams, just the double of 1980. Some twenty four countries participated in the period. Japan accounted for 141 national and 8 joint expeditions out of a total of 404 teams in the third decade. The United Kingdom sent 30, West Germany 28, France 27, U.S.A. 25, Austria 20, Italy 19, Spain and Poland 15 each. Nine were from Switzerland and Seven from South Korea. Czechoslavakia and Yogoslavia each sent six expeditions. Australia, Canada and the Netherlands had for expedition each. Bulgaria, Iran, and Mexico were new entrants with one expedition each. Nepal itself launched its first expedition on the border peak.

All eight thousanders with the exception of Cho oyu were climbed many times. Sagarmatha (Mount Everest) was ascended sixteen times-twice in 1973, 1974, 1978, 1979 and 1980 and thrice in 1976. The highlight of expedition of Sagarmatha can be summarized in the following way :

— To celebrate the 200th anniversary of the American Independence, the American Bicentennial Expedition Scaled Sagarmatha on October 1976 under the leadership of Phel Trimble.

— The first Sagarmatha International Expedition 1971 which compressed of 12 Nations was meant to develop the Universal brotherhood.

— Joint British Nepal Army Expedition team scaled Sagarmatha.

— Mr. Junko Tabei, first women-scaled Sagarmatha in 1975 on the occassion of International Women's year. The Chinese Miss Phantog and other 8 persons on the same occasion.

— His Majesty's Government, Ministry of Tourism celebrated Nepal Mountaineers week to mark the silver Jubilee of Sagarmatha weak in May 29, June 4, 1978.

— His Majesty's Government published Mountaineering Expedition Regulation 2036 (1979).

— The Kathmandu Declaration on Mountain Activities-UIAA, (The International Union of Alpinist Associations met in Kathmandu, 1982).

All eight thousanders with the exception of Cho oyu were climbed many times. Sagarmatha (Mountain Everest) was climbed sixteen times. Manaslu was scaled ten times Mukalu, Dhaulgiri and Annapurna I were all climbed eight times. Kanchanjunga and Lhotse six times each. Ama Dablam and Pumori climbed with seven ascents, Jaunu five times and Yalung Kang four times respectfully. Fourth decade of Mountaineering (1981 to the present).

In 1980-90 there were too many expeditions to list in detail. During the year 1990 alone, as many as 120 expeditions attempted to scale different peaks of the Nepal Himalayas. For 1991, approximately 130 expedition teams have been given permission to scale different peaks.

Since His Majesty's Government, Nepal, Ministry of Tourism adopted liberal policy in mountaineering in early 1980's there has been steady growth to mountaineering activities in the Nepal Himalaya. This has motivated the zeal of mountaineers of the world for climbing satellite summits lesser peaks and attempting new routes. Some of the peaks previously been closed to foreigners were opened. Peaks previously unnamed were given new names. His Majesty's Government has opened eight new peaks in the western side of the Nepal Himalayas in 1992, bringing the total number of peaks above 6,000 meters open to climbing to 222.

Recently, His Majesty Government has opened Mount Dragnag Ri (6801 m), Mount Gyaji Kang (7038 m), Mount Givigela (7350 m), Mount Pathibhara (7125 m) and Mount Lang

Po Peak (6954 m) in Dolkha, Manang, Taplejung and Taplejung respectively.

A glimpse of mountaineering expedition in 1994, the total number of expedition teams was 19 in the spring season and 9 different peaks were successfully climbed by 13 teams. Khumbu Region was popular and attracted more than 47 percent of total mountaineering activity. To diverse pressure from Khumbu, His Majesty Government has taken pressure from Khumbu, His Majesty Government has taken measures on Mt. Everest. Under the new regulations the royalty fee for climbing Sagarmatha has been fixed up to US $50,000 from US $10,000. Similarly, only one expedition will be granted permission per route on the world's highest mountain. HMG/ Ministry of Tourism has also introduced summer season for climbing from 1993, formerly only three mountaineering season. HMG/Ministry of Tourism in responsible to issue permission for expedition desirous for climbing any of the mountain peaks declared open.

Mountaineering is one of the important aspect of adventure tourism in Nepal as well as the major source of foreign exchange earning of the country.

TREKKING

Trekking tourism exhibits the most outstanding type of tourism in Nepal and sets forth a positive trend in demand. Nepal unfolds unique Himalayan attractions with rich culture personating an element of touristic interest such, as the people, their religious shrines, ancient movement, art treasures and festivals and national splendours resulting from physical, climatic and ecological features. While these attractions and values set up the essential ingredients for the development of trekking tourism and their economic turn up is obtained from the economic utilisation of these resources. While realising these views, Nepal has developed trekking tourism in all areas of wilderness of the country.

Trekking as really the most enjoyable part of tourism in Nepal. There are many remote and wild unspoilt areas which have potential attractions for trekking tourism. Trekking trail passes on the most beautiful and charming landscapes as nature has bestowed to make Nepal as 'Shangrila'. In order to familiar with the natural beauty at the close angle and the cultural diversity of the people the visitor must go in trekking. The only way to get acquainted with the people, their way of life, their culture, the singular scenic beauties is trekking in Nepal.

Trekking in Nepal is not a wildman back-packing experience but a means of transportation to get from one mountain village to another through a terrain where vehicles can not go. Nepal offers various forms of trekking. Trekking provides an opportunity and a thrilling charm by the magnificance of affluence of attractive natural beauty at every step in the terrain of mountain slopes, viewing lakes, rushing streams and rivers, rolling green countrysides and the warm hearted and hospitable people everywhere which add relaxation more exhilerating and comfortable.

Trekking in Nepal can provide an opportunity to see and enjoy such wonders as deepest gorges, snowy peaks, glacier moraines, waterfalls, rocky as well as green hills, national parks and the best of other famous places and sights. No other country offers so many features within a short distance of trekking.

There are various types of treks in the mountain areas of Nepal. Trekking tours, are, therefore, very wide in scope and organised on the basis of the interest of trekkers. Trekking in the Himalayan slopes up to an altitude of 5,500 m is within the scope of ordinary tourist and has developed rapidly as a major activity. Many restricted parts of the Himalayas have also been opened to foreignes for trekking recently. Trekking is, therefore at the moment concentrated in the Kathmandu/Langtang/ Everest and the Jomsom/Pokhara/Annapurna areas. Certain parts of the Himalayas and 'restricted' and not open to foreigners trekking. Subject to over coming these restrictions, trekking has now been extended to various previously restricted Himalayan regions of Nepal.

There are many licensed trekking agencies which provide a full range of trekking equipment, catering facilities including trekking guides and trekking cooks. Special treks are designed for individuals or groups interested in bird-watching, trekking combined with white-water rafting, wildlife safari and observing cultural activities of the common folk, cannoeing in the snow-fed rivers and streams and bathing in the hot spring etc.

Trekking is categorised into two main forms of short and long duration and it usually covers four regions of the Himalaya as

1. Northern Region
2. Central Region
3. Eastern Everest Region
4. Western Region

The most short and popular trekking is also possible by going around the rim of hills of the Kathmandu valley or around the city of Pokhara. A short trek is designed to give the trekker a brief taste of some major peaks of scenic attractions of particular regions generally involving four to eight days of walking with the starting point being Lukla for the Everest Region and Pokhara for Annapurna and Gorepani. The first of the most popular trekking regions is around the Mount Everest in the East and' Pokhara/ Annapurna to the west. Larger treks involve more complex itineraries such as that to and around Everest Base Camp or to Manang, Jomsom. Along is usually scheduled for between 23 or 30 days and organised for more experienced and physically sound adventurers.

A trekking permit is a must for all foreigners to trek in Nepal. Visa extension will also be required if the duration of the trek is likely to exceed the 30 days from the Central Immigration Office, Kathmandu. Two passport size photographs are required for the permit. Authorised trekking agencies will be able to provide all information, equipment and personnel required for trekking. The trekking season in Nepal commences in September each year and ends in May.

Nepal is famous world-wide for its scenic mountain treks. One of the best ways in which to explore and enjoy the country as a whole, is trekking. It is advisable to make trekking arrangements through a reputable trekking agency which can provide reliable guides, equipment and personalised services. The most popular trekking routes are listed below for ever increasing flow of trekkers to there areas due to their matchless scenery and unspoiled beauty of the ancient culture, life style of mountain villages and tropical, sub-tropical forest to high snowy mountain peaks:

1. Northern Region : *i.e.* to the north of Kathmandu, mainly Helambu, Gosainkunda, Langtang Valley and Ganesh Himal etc.

(a) Helambu—This valley is famous for its natural beauty and wonderful climate. The snow-covered mountains such as Gosainthan, Langtang Lirung and Jugal Himal can be seen from the trail in their superb grandeur. Helambu is about 72 kms. north of Kathmandu and covers typical lighland Sherpa villages. This region extends from the north to Taramarang to the Gosainkunda Lake and the lower Jugal Himal from the north. The valley is approached from the Trisuli valley, north of Kathmandu. The trek is usually for 8 days.

(b) Gosainkunda—It is situated at an altitude 5,100 m to the north-west of Helambu and 132 kilometers north-east of Kathmandu. This is a sacred place of Hindu Pilgrimage. The trekking route to Gosainkunda, which requires 15 to 20 days. The place is famous for beautiful landscape, glacial lakes, waterfalls and evergreen forests.

(c) The Langtang Valley—This valley is covered by mountains and glaciers at an altitude of 3000 meters and is north to Gosainkunda. It is one of the most enchanting and scenic spots of Nepal. There are many Yak pastures available

for camping sites. There is also the Langtang National Park to view the Himalayan flora and fauna. This park is the home to musk deer, snow leopard, Himalayan black bear, and black buck etc. The Langtang village is a remarkable place of loveliness in the backdrop of the Lirung Himal. There is also a cheese factory established with the Swiss technical help. This trek takes 14 days.

(d) The Ganesh Himal—This trekking provides unusual sights of the traditional life style of the people and unspoilt wilderness. The trekking commences from Syaubru Bensi to Chilime Khola with a attractive panorama of the Ganesh Himal. This trek is for 17 days. The trekking permit and guide are necessary.

2. Central Region—The gateway to all trekking areas around central region is Pokhara, the lake district of Nepal and the secondary tourist destination after Kathmandu valley. Short treks from Pokhara cover Nou Danda, Ghorepani, Tatopani, Rupse Chhahara etc. Nau Danda is a very good look out point to see the lovely view of the Pokhara valley with the Phewa Lake and the attractive peaks of Annapurna. Ghorepani is situated amidst rhododendrun forests and the majestic peaks of Dhaulagiri Himal can be seen from here. Tatopani is known for its hot spring and the Rupse Chhahara Fall is one of the best waterfall in this region.

(a) Jomsom—This place is full of Thakali settlements and looks Tibet with its bare mountains slopes and countryside. The whole upper Kali Gandaki valley beyond Ghasa to Marpha is covered by Thak villages, monasteries, pine woods, snowfed streams and barely fields. It takes 12 days for this trek one can make side treks to the famous shrine at Muktinath Dana, Lete and Kagheni. The trek is famous for providing exellent view for the impressive peaks of the Dhaulagiri and Annapurna Himalayan ranges.

(b) Muktinath—It lies near about 18 kilometers north-east of Jomson. This famous place of pilgrimage is located in the vast and dry rain shadow of the Himalayas. This trek starts

from Pokhara via Bydam, Sarankot, Tirkhedunge and Ghorepani. From Gorepani, trek descends into the valley of the sacred Kali Gandaki and the trek route passes through the heart of the mountains carved by the valley of the Kali Gandaki and the deepest gorge in the world. After Tatopani, the treacherous trail finished and heads on to the north. Then the route passes through Dana and Titre and the vegetation thins and the path becomes steeper with the view of boulder-strewn and cataract filled gorge. The climb passes with marvellous sight of the high falls of Rupse Chhahara. The trek follows to trail to Marpha and turns off for the route to Muktinath. The importance of Muktinath as a pilgrimage place for the Hindus abounds in sacred Saligrams as the emblem of Narayan. There is a small pagoda temple of Jwala Mai equally worshipped both by the Hindu and Buddhists alike. Surrounding the temple a stone wall encircles one hundred and eight bull head shaped brass water spouts. The trek to Muktinath proceeds through the Thorang Pass and is difficult due to lack of water and camping sites. It takes about 15 days to trek this route. This trek covers the "Thak" area. The Thakali villages are very picturesque and their architecture of the houses is quite typical with fire-wood piled on their roofs. Trekking permit and guide necessary.

(c) Manang—Manang is located to the north of the Annapurna range and is a valley situated in a high altitude. It can be trekked following the way of Muktinath or along the Marsyangdi river of Langtang. The appropriate starting point for this trek is Dumre, 1,350 feet up to Manang, the Marsyandi valley at an altitude of 11,600 feet has to be crossed.

Manang presents a very impressive image and it is located completely isolated by the barrier of the Lamjung and Annapurna massifs. The trek follows a few forests and pastures and full of barren rocky slopes and rugged stony areas. The ethnic and cultural attractions are many as the Marsyandi valley is populated by Lamaist Buddhists. Many Gompas, Buddhist monasteries, along the way having age old art treasures are found. This trek can be done from eight to ten days.

(d) Annapurna I, Annapurna Sanctuary and Around Annapurna—Trek to the Annapurna I region of around Annapurna Base Camp takes 22 days. This trek is popular as a classic trek and covers a circuit trip of the Annapurna range by passing all types of attractive panorama. This trek starts from the low altitude with rice fields and slowly comes across medieval looking villages on way to Manang. The highest spot, the Throng La pass, is 5,398 m. The trekker has a majestic view of Annapurna II, III, IV and Gangapurna traversing down the Kali Gandaki, the deepest gorge in the world. There is even a fair chance to view Dhaulagiri, 8167 m peak. This circuitous trek begins at Dumre, halfway to Pokhara, up to the Manang valley, over to Muktinath and down Jomsom back to Pokhara with a trip to the Annapurna sanctuary to see a great variety of people, places and cultural festivities.

Annapurna Sancturay is world famous place to view various Himalayan mountains such as Annapurna, Gangpurna, Glacier Dome and Macchapuchare in close range without strenuous, prolonged trek before hand.

The trail passes through rhododendron and bamboo forests and the Gurung village of Handring and Ghanring. The high point of the trek is 3,731 m—a miracle of mountain amphitheatre. Trek to Annapurna sancturay takes 16 days and around Annapurna 22 days. Annapurna base camp trek takes its course from Chandrakot leaving aside the Jhomusmli trail and enjoying best views of the majestic Himalayan panorama.

(e) Around Dhaulagiri—This is also a difficult trek. It takes around 23 days. This trek also starts from Pokhara amidst cultivated fields and passes through the rhododendron and alpine fórests and meadows with high routes with plenty of landscape of mountain views.

3. Eastern Region—Popular as Everest Region—This trek compasses not only the Everest Base Camp but also Namche Bazar, Lukla, Thanghoche and the whole Solukhumbu area at the background of Mount Everest, the highest peak in the world. The Everest trek as is popularly-known is in the

Khumbu region and has been long associated with the various Everest expeditions.

This trek is of approximately 300 miles and covers 25 to 30 days depending more or less on the stamina of the trekker. The trail passes through Phaphlu, a very lovely Sherpa village to Jumbesi to Salleri and to the Buddhist monastery at Chiwong. Lukla—another famous place as the gateway to the Everest region and then to Namche Bazar, situated at 3475 m. After a days walk, one can reach the spiritual centre of the whole Sherpa land—the Buddhist monastery at Thyangboche. Above Namche Bazar just about one hour's trek, the trekker can reah at the highest resort hotel, Everest View Hotel. This is an accommodation service situated in the highest place in the world. This hotel is very close to two Sherpa villages of Kunde and Khumjung.

All areas of the Khumbu region are within the Sagarmatha National Park. The Everest Region is marvellous due to its extra-ordinary mountainscape and the friendly and hospitable Sherpa people who are famous as the tiger of the snows and no mountaineering expeditions are successful without their assistance and help. This trek is very lovely due to beautiful panorama, lots of ups and downs, scenic rivers and rhododendrons and fine forests. Variety of scenery and ethic groups are on the trail. The trail passes through rice areas and the tea plantation region of Illam, middle foothills and high peaks. The Everest trek takes 16 days.

Eastern Region has famous for the following treks :

(a) Chautara "Rhododendron Trek—13 days in all. A wonderful 14 days trek for viewing wildflowers, snow-capped peaks, all in the north of Nepal. This trek is known as easy trek.

(b) Rolwaling Himal Trek—A difficult trek for the healthy and adventurers with valleys, moraines, glaciers and passes of the Solu Khumbu and a visit to Thami, home of the legendary Sherpa-Tenzing Norgey. It takes 23 days.

(c) The Hongu Valley Trek—This trek is arduous but the most interesting of all treks in the Khumbu region. The duration of this trek in 22 days.

(d) Ganja-La trek—This 20 days trek—This is top grade trek for the fit and adventurers.

Eastern Kanchanjunga Trek

This trek is equally enjoyable and memorable. It usually requires 25 days. Kanchanjunga is 8,598 m high peak and its dazzling summits are of astonishing beauty and charm. This area is newly opened for trekkers in 1988. This trekking area is only allowed to trek through the authorized trekking agents. The trekking starts from Kathmandu to Mulghat on the plains of the Terai. The traits of Eastern Nepal pass on the Tamur Kosi river side with ethnic groups such as Rai, Limbu, Tamang and others living on the lovely villages. The views of Kanchunjunga, Makalu and Jannu Himal are beautiful also through the trekking routes. The route comes to Illam the final place to return to Kathmandu by bus.

4. Western Region—Western regions has wonderful places like Surkhet, Jumla and Rara lake and Dolpa.

Jumla is located at an altitude of 2,340 m. and consists of forested foothills of pines, Juniper and Spruce. Lake Rara National Park is neary 28 kilometers far from the main Jumla Bazar which is airlinked with Kathmandu. From Jumla, first the trail passes through Pandmara village and then to the Crest of Dori Lekh following the Khali Lagna pass, Ghurchi Lagna, Pima, Thkurgaun and the western point of the lake is reached. Lake Rara is also reached from Dhorpattan in the north-west of the Pokhara valley but this is a difficult 15 days trek through fifteen thousand feet altitude via Jangla Bhanjyang to Tar. About 6 miles from Tar, the Thuli Bheri river is set aside and it follows the right bank of the Suli-river which joins into the Bheri river from the north via Danhi and to Rara Lake.

Dolpa Region

This trek takes 24 days. Dolpa is full of Tibetan landscape and it is a hermit land full of devoted Buddhists. The valley is considered to be created by Guru Padmasambhava as a refuge for ardent Buddhists long times ago. Dolpa area is preserved by the Shey Phoksundo National Park covering 3555 sq. kilometers, one of the Nepal's largest natural conservation park. This region has an unspoiled natural environment and typical culture of its own amidst Tibetan like landscape. The Shey Phoksundo National Park is the home of blue sheep, the rarest animal in the world. The Himalayan black bear, leopard, wolf and snow leopard are also found here. The maximum altitude of this trek is 5,115 m. In order to trek the Dolpa region it is recommended to fly to Nepalgunj in the southern Terai from Kathmandu and then Dolpa by flight from Nepalgunj.

Trekking tourism in Nepal is an exciting experience. It instals an appreciation of unspoiled countryside, wonderful natural surroundings lush green alpine valleys, terraced fields steeping up on hillsides, rushing rivers and streams, deep gorges, emerald lakes, flower decorated meadows in the backdrop of snow. To get the most out of visit to Nepal, a trek into the Himalayan foothills is almost an enjoyment and relaxation.

Recently more trekking destinations hitherto restricted are open in different parts of the country and a trekker can trek in these areas after receipt of prior approval of the Ministry of Home, His Majesty's Government of Nepal. These areas can be trekked by a foreigner only through the dealing with a registered trekking agency. These newly opened areas for trekking cover 50 village development Committees spread over 13 districts bordering the Tibet Autonomous Region of China. Among these opened areas include highly attractive of singular landscapes places like Olangchunggola in Tablejung, Kimanthanka in Sankhuwasabha, Lomanthang in Mustang, among others equally potential places.

Trekking can be undertaken by any person of sound physical build-up who merely seeks recreation without under bodily hazards, deserves only the relaxation afforded by the isolated mountain valleys. Unilike mountaineering expedition, it can be done by any person who loves nature in its pristine glory and no professional skill as in mountaineering is needed for it.

There are mountain peaks, however are designated as trekking peaks having 5,000 to 6,635 m. for adventure trekkers. These peaks consist of 18 numbers and are opened for trekking parties with previous permissioin from the Nepal Mountaineering Association by paying royalty prescribed to each and every peaks. The details of the peaks are as follows:

Name of Peak	Altitude in Meters	Location
Chulu West	6,630	Centre
Mera Peak I	6,431	East
Fluted Peak	6,390	Centre-West
Kusum Kangro	6,369	East
Hiunchuli	6,337	Centre-West
Pharchamo	6,282	Centre-West
Chulu East	6,200	Centre
Kwangde	6,194	East
Island Peak	6,153	East
Lobuche Peak	6,119	East
Pisang Peak	6,091	Centre-West
Ramdung Peak	6,021	Centre-West
Paldor Peak	5,894	Centre
Mera Peak II	5,820	East
Ganjala Chuli	5,806	Centre
Pokhalde Peak	5,806	East
Mardi Himal	5,555	Centre-West
Tent Peak	5,500	Centre-West

WHITE-WATER RAFTING

The white-water rafting is really a captivating travel experience in Nepal. Rafting offers an unforgettable thrill in travel where the visitor discovers endless variety of beauty—the ageless enchantments of the picturesque valley, serene and Kalidoscopic colours and forms of the Himalayan massifs in the horizon, the colourful charm displayed by row of country's avifauna and the flora in line with unspolit culture and life style of the rural folk.

There are many rivers in Nepal suitable for rafting. Rafting voyage will begen in the deep mountain valley gorges upstream and conclude in the downstream of the Terai plains. Rafting is all season sport and just one of many unique adventure exclusive to Nepal. During the summer months (May, June and July) the river levels are extremely high due to snow melt and the monsoon rains. These months are considered the most difficult for rafting. September through March are the best months for the rafter. Rafting in the rivers of Nepal during winter is a suitable time which creates the most interesting and varied pattern in the world-thickly forested valley through rock, gorges into open sub-tropical plans—all in a few days. To the ardent adventurer, rafting in the stomy rivers of Nepal keeps nerve tingling rapture of strange and wonderful feeling. The exiting depth of the snow-fed rivers of Nepal cut by tectonic convulsion and flowing through the continued bending in turbulent flow, all create marvel of excitement and bewilder.

The development of white-water rafting has taken place over the last few years in Nepal. It is scientifically and commercially established at present. It has become popular adventure sport in Nepal. The first move for its development was made in 1974 by the three adventurous Germans who explored the rivers of Nepal. Since then, the rivers of Nepal is attracting many rafters because of the large number of wild, untrained waves in them. The rivers provide difficult obstacles and no two rivers are the same. Many rivers are wilderness areas and floating through a steep river raft a broad river valley through lush forest land of Terai can be quite exciting.

White-water rafting trips take plae in the various snow-fed rivers of Nepal such as Trisuli, Narayani, Marsyangdi, Seti and Sunkoshi. Easily accessible places from Kathmandu valley are the Sunkoshi and Trisuli rivers, because of their convenient location and they are the most frequent rafted rivers in Nepal. Except Trisuli, other rivers mentioned above provide the opportunity for longer rafting trips whereas the river Trisuli is excellent for one or two or three day programme. Rafting trips consist of one day to several days longer trips. It is organised by many agencies as a growing part of an integral part of mountain tourism. They offer combined trips of trekking and rafting—as for example trip down the Trisuli river to Royal Chitwan National Park in the southern lowland Terai followed by a two or three day stay at one of the Park's hotels or lodges. These agencies organise float and raft trips on the different rivers of Nepal lasting 1 day to 15 days or more. They own rubber rafts and trained raftsmen. Rafting trip can be done in many side conyons, tributary streams, gorges and villages which provide good occasions for photography and for the exploration and enjoyment of the river valley ecosystem.

River Rafting was introduced by Himalayan river Excursion in 1977. Eight rivers in the three river systems are open for tourists for river rafting. The rivers are the Trisuli, the Kaligandaki, the Bheri, the Seti, the Sankosi, Karnali, Tamakosi and the Arun. Among these rivers, Trisuli, Sankosi, Tamor, Bhotesori, Arun Karnali, Kaligandaki, Bheri and Seti are popular rivers for white-water rafting. Of them, Trisuli is the most popular and most crowded.

The most popular long rafting trip is ten-day Sunkosi river run. It is a strange and turbulent river and the rafting can be done only by tough rafters and experienced guides. There are now more rivers for rafting such as Bheri river which takes its course through Royal Bardia National Park. Other rivers such as Arun and Karnali are also equally used for river rafting. The Arun and Karnali rivers are very wild and so are good to be used by professional rafters and due to their isolated position of reaching there and to return back. Rafting and canoeing provides a taste of hair raising adventure and excitement.

Group rates for white-water rafting vary and depend on group size and trip duration. Rafting on the Arun river, on the tributary of the Sapta Koshi in eastern Nepal, the Narayani in Central Nepal, the Karnali in far western Nepal and the Mahakali in Western Nepal offer the most exciting and exhilerating experience. The visitor will find the experience in Nepal most enchanting while rafting in the torrential rivers of Nepal.

GLIDING

Gliding is introduced into Nepal recently. The air-borne sports which have introduced from abroad, include balloning, gliding and para-gliding.

Gliding means to travel through the air without expenditure of power. Glider means one who or that which glides an aircraft like an aeroplane without engine. This is the sport of flying in a glider. Gliding aircraft is made of synthetic nylon or polyamade which flies without mechanical propulsion. Gliding requires the slope along which gliding is made to come in for flying and landing. It is a sport to go stealthily or gradually by utilising air currents.

Para-gliding is also a sport of being towed through the air then allowed to drift to the gound. This is a form of streerable parachute, consisting of air-filled nylon cells. A glider flies in the air with inflatable wings. It was firstly started in Nepal on 1990. Many Nepali people now well trained in the art of paragliding.

There are many good places in Nepal for both sports of gliding and para-gliding. There are mountain slopes rising up to the valleys in various places. These mountain slopes offer best places for the flying and the valley below for landing. A trip by flying by means of gliding and para-gliding for viewing the panorama of changing scenery, the rugged mountains, the timbered slopes to the wide sweep of the rivers is full of excitements and entertainment. All the programmes of gliding and para-gliding are organised in a places which are most suitable for such sports in the very heart of Nepal's scenic wonderland. These sports are immensely helpful to view green landscape that bask under the big sky, mountain ranges that circle it glacier-carrying Himalayan peaks that pierce its fluffy clouds unspoiled scenery, restful villages and other fascinating attractions. These sports are organised by registered agencies in prior information.

MOUNTAIN BICYCLING

The travel programme of mountain bicycling is also introduced quite recently. It is the newest addition to adventure travel sports in the country. Nepal is the first country in South Asia to bring this sport to the region.

Mountain bicycling has gained wide popularity in U.S.A. Europe and Australia. This is apart form being a healthy exercise by body built up, it provides relief from the hub of the modern life, relaxing the mind and body of tension of urban stress while making contact with nature closely.

Mountain travel on bicycling can cause the traveller to experience the natural beauty of Nepal when he likes. It is easy to explore the outskirts of Kathmandu and beyond the Kathmandu valley and causes a rare thrill, a travel experience "of the beaten track". The traveller can ride along the bank of the cool green rivers and can stop for a swim or can ride to remote temple and shrines and can stop at will to explore them. It can be ride over mountain passes and can stop to praise majestic Himalayan panorama and can ride through jungle and stop for a relaxation or wildlife watching. Mountain biking is an adventure in itself which allows to enjoy at one's own pace.

Nepal is mountain biker's dreamland. A bicycling down the narrow and stone path of the tri-cities of the Kathmandu valley can be enthralling, because life there is and the ambience of centuries past. It provides endless paved, dirt to trails on the mountain terrains. Biking along these routes can be challenging as well as entertaining.

Bicycle can be hired for leisurely rides around the narrow streets of the Kathmandu valley's cities. It is good for short tour. A popular mode of transport is the bicycle which is easily rented. It provides opportunity to mingle with the local people or doing a brisk walk.

Mountain biking trips organised in Nepal are in accordance with the will of the visitor. It is organised to suit novices and professionals. The length of the trips offen depends upon the willingness of the traveller with only a few hours or to pass several days on bicycle on the rim of the mountain terrain. There is bicycling programme arranged up to the starting place to river-rafting or to a high altitude trek starting point.

There is no shortage of things to do in Nepal for the energetic but if one does not favour a long trek or jungle safari, these is no lack either of cultural attractions both past and present which can be enjoyed by a short bicycle trip in Nepal. The visitor can combine trips on bicycle with mountain viewing as opposed to mountain climbing, choosing from a variety of vantage points and historical towns throughout Nepal.

The agencies licenced to organise tours offer the services of trained guides, eighteen gear mountain bicycle in the best conditions, with driving helmet, rack pack, all meals and if need requires accommodations as well.

HOT-AIR BALLONING

This sport is firstly introduced by International trekkers of Nepal and Adventure Travel Centre of Australia as a joint venture in Nepal recently. They have joined hand to make Asia first commercial hot-air ballonging programme in Nepal. This sport is now popular among the visitors and is sure to create new tourist interest in the country. This is the latest in the list of adventure programme that have been introduced since Nepal opened its door to travellers in 1950.

Hot-air ballon consists of a bag of plastic material inflated with a gas lighter than air. The inflated sphere of plastic material is supported by a large envelope of gas lighter than air. This airship like ballon derives its lift from a large bag inflated with a gas which is lighter than air outside. The ballon goes for travel in the air consisting of a gas-bag and a car. The ballon goes up making use of heated air which is forced to compensate for changes of pressure in the gas-bag. The ballon goes high in the air. It is used as a hobby by a number of enthusiasts.

Hot-air balloning is so popular in Nepal that the four balloonists even ventured to fly over Sagarmatha (Mount Everest) in the ballon. Two adventurists Chris Dewhirst of Australia and Leo Dickenson from Britain firstly flew over in one hot-air ballon and they were followed by Endy Elson and Eric Jones in another. The hot-air ballon was started from Gokyo in the Gokyo valley, some 15 kilometers west of the Everest Base camp and flew over 87 degrees into Rongxar in the Tibetan Plateau. This was the first hot-air balloning to the highest mountain in the earth, Mount Everest 8848 m. Many enthusiasts from Brirtain and Japan also tried this adventurous sport but they were not able to successful due to the bad weather.

Hot-air balloning a newly introduced adventure activity in Nepal. Ballon sunrise Nepal experience provides unique sensation of being suspended between earth and sky moving slowly over the picturesque Kathmandu valley. The panoramic profile of the surrounding mountains are unbelievable.

MOUNTAIN MARATHON

Mountain marathon signifies marathonian or marathon race—a long distance foot race from Kathmandu to any Base camp of the Nepal Himalayas. It displays powers of endurance and stamina as welll as test of endurance of great length in time and distance. Even since the concept of high altitude race was thought of in the form of Everest International Marathon in Nepal, this response has been immense. There has been participants from many parts of the world. Mountain marathon provides new and refreshing experience. This mountain race is fascinating, chilling, challenging and adventurous. It is recommended to climbers for trekking in any of the trekking peaks, some experience in mountain climbing and use of equipments are necessary.

Trekking tourism in particular has emerged not only as a

leading but also a distinctive type of tourism with an ample opportunity in building up an independent market for Nepal. Nepal provides all sort of trekking possibilites from difficult treks which may ascend above 5,500 meters to shorter treks at lesser altitudes around the mountain valleys themselves. Organised treks range from a few days of gentle walking around a scenically attractive area such as Pokhara to two or more months the high-altitude mountaineering and glacier scrambling that would be tough even for professionals. One of the results of the general trends towards the bigger development and increased popularity of 'adventure' tourism within Asia over recent years has been the boom in trekking in Nepal. There are 342 licenced trekking agencies providing services to the international visitors.

Sporting Tourism—This has two different aspects. First, there are the big sports meetings like the Olympics Games, the continental or world Ski, football, boxing championships etc. which attract to the country not only the sportsman concerned but also thousands of followers and interested people.

On the other hand, there is what can be called the sporting Tourism of the Devotees. Winter sports, natural sports mountain climbing, horse riding, hunting, fishing sports, countries which are well placed to develop certain of these sports also have the good fortune to attract many devotees and thus benefit from this type of tourism.

Nepal has fairly established as a good place for adventure and sport tourism. This has amply proved by the increasing flux of international visitors for trekking, white-water rafting, wildlife safari, mountaineering and many other sports.

6

WILD-LIFE TOURISM

Nepal is nature lover's paradise. It is a very small country but has a diversion of differences due to its topography. Physically, it presents a contrasting image. The northern fringe is dotted with the highest peaks in the world. Mount Everest (8848 m) the world's towering peak, dominates the amphitheatre of Himalayan peaks and tiers of hills. The trans-Himalayan Valley, over 3,658 m above sea level has an extremely dry climate, sparse vegetation and is marginal in terms of human habitation. The climate is alpine. These heights are full of alpine meadows, pine ridges to temperate rain forests full of common rhododendrons. Its midland zone (above 1,822 m) cut across by snow fed rivers forms some of the deepest gorges in the world. In this zone roughly 52 percent of the Nepal population live. The area of the lowland Terai is played up by the deep and silent rivers which cascade down the mountain gorges carrying their milk white icy waters.

Nepal has tropical, sub-tropical and alpine climates with natural differences in its flora and fauna within its small compass. In the Terai, Sal (Sorea Robusta), Sissau, Acacia grow in abundance. The inner Terai Savannah forests are full to tall grass and bamboo. In the middle Himalayan zone or the hill country region, the climate is temperate where pines, rhododendrons, elms, poplars, walnuts and willow predominate. In the higher Himalayas—oaks, maples and pines grow and in the alpine zone Junipers, short rhododendrons and varieties of medicinal herbs.

Along with the varied vegetations, Nepal has a varied and rich species of fauna. Variety of species of wildlife available in the forests of Nepal. These include the wild buffaloes, snow leopard, black bucks, wild elephants, antelopes, one-horned rhinoceros, tigers, bears, musk deers, blue sheeps, stags, red panda etc.

Nepal is also a repository of many species of birds, fishes, reptiles amphibians and insects. About 830 species of birds sucha as pheasants, snow pigeon, snow patridges, golden eagle, kalig pheasant, chakor tragopan, yellow billed chough and many others are found here. The Danphey (Lophophorous) is the country's national bird. Many migratory birds are seen in the slopes and in the river banks. Dolphin and crocodile are abound in the rivers of the Terai. The variety and availability of fauna increase progressively with decreasing altitude and increasing luxuriance of the vegetation.

This sketch described above is suffice to show what of vast collection of flora and fauna this rich country is to the lover of wild animal and bird life, to the naturalist and to the lover of nature. So two Natinal Parks *i.e.,* Everest National Park (1148 sq. kms.) and Royal Chitwan Natural Park (1932 sq. kms.) are listed in World Heritage Sites (Natural) by UNESCO.

NATIONAL PARKS AND WILD-LIFE RESERVES

Due to geographical location and great altitudinal range, Nepal displays a great diversity of physical features and climate. So flora and fauna of Nepal comprise an important part of Nepal's natural heritage. Nepal, with its pre-eminent range of altitude (from 152 m) above the sea level in the Terai in the south to more than 8848 m in the north Himalayas, its plain preserving identity from rich alluvial areas to bare crystalline rocks and its rainfall from 60 to 100 inches on the outer ranges to nearly a tenth of that amount behind the great mountains, has an amazing range and variety of both flora and fauna.

The altitude variation requires a division of the country into three natural regions:

1. Himalayan Region: This lies art an altitude of 4877 m to 8848 m above the sea level with the snow line running at 4877

m. The Himalayan summits like the Kumbhakarna, the Jugal, the Mustang, the Ganesh, the Annapurna, Cho-oyu and Machhapuchhre fan out from the east to west. In this region, the world's famous peaks of Mount Everest (8848 m), Kanchanjunga (8586 m), Dhaulagiri (8,167 m) and Annapurna (8,091 m) are settled enchanting characteristic details of particular scenery. Establishment of National Parks at this regions have been able to protect the rich natural heritage in great numbers. Listed below are the National Parks established in this regions:

(a) Sagarmatha (Mount Everest) National Park

This park was gazetted in 1976 and extends 1,1,48 sq. kms. of geological interest containing Everest and lying above 3,500 m altitude. It is an example of high region ecology. Besides, its spectacular scenery, it is the habitat of musk-deer Himalayan Thar, Ibex and other Himalayan species. This is included in the World Heritage list of UNESCO. Snow Leopard and Yeti, the snow man are also believed to live in this park. Blood pheasant and Impeyan pheasant are common scene around Namache and Thangboche areas. Other species of birds as blood pheasant, snow pigeon, Tibetan snow cock and Himalayan griffon are also found in the park.

This park is located in the valley of Imja Khola which lies in the north-eastern region of Nepal in Solu Khumbu district. The vegetations of the lower valleys consist of blue pine, fir and juniper forests. Juniper and rhododendron trees can be seen up to 4,700 meters. There are also carnivorous animals like the Himalayan wolf and black bear in the park.

Solu Khumbu is the land of Sherpa. It is a magnificient and fascinating area. No mountaineering expedition can be successful without their cooperation and assistance of Sherpa—known as the tiger of the snow. The park also includes many Sherpa villages which have considered as a part of ecosystem and of cultural resource. The landscapes of the park is unique as here are the highest mountains in the world, snow-capped, rock-faced, these mountains rise, proud and unchallenged, mass on mass. The combination of snow, rock and ice can be responsible for some of Nature's most exciting scenery. Sherpas rear upon Yaks, their beasts of burden. The park also contain many Gompas of religious importance.

The access to the park is by flying to a altiport at Lukla, about two day's walk from Namche Bazar, the principal village within the park or by trekking from the south via the Dudh Kosi Valley. There are facilities of lodges, Park Headquarters and visitor centre at Namche.

(b) Shey Phoksundo National Park

A Trans-Himalayan area in Dolpa district of north-western Nepal and the landscape is typically Tibetan with similar vegetations and wildlife. It covers 3,555 sq. kms. It was established in 1984. The main attraction of the park is the magnificent lake Phoksundo or also known by another name Ringmo lake. The southern side of the lake has got smooth lands with grass which are good for camping sites. The south-eastern parts of the lake are covered with the forests of pines and junipers. There is a beautiful monastery in the forest. There is an ideal village at the southern part of the lake. This lake derives its name out of the cultivated village named as Ringmo village. The most spectacular sight in the Dolpo region is the attractive waterfalls (550 feet) which is the drain of Lake Ringmo.

This park has wildlife species of large population of blue sheep, Himalayan tahr, Himalayan black Bear, ghoral, serow, common leopard, Himalayan marmots, snowcock, Himalayan weasel, wolf, snow leopard and other characteristic species.

The park can be reached via Rara lake or Dhorpatan and the trek is classic walk for 10 days one way. It can be reached 3 to 4 days trek from Dunche.

(c) Rara National Park

This national park is located in the remote north-west region of the country in Karnali zone. It covers 106 sq. kms. of scenic beauty and representative ecology of the forested part of northwest. It lies at an altitude between 2,990 and 4038 m. The vegetations within the park are consisited of typical mixed forests but conifers predominate. It includes Lake Rara, Nepal's largest lake and is an important resting place for migrating waterfowl. It is an luxurious valley with green meadows, forested foot-hills of pine, juniper and spruce in the background of a panorama of Himalayan snow peaks. There is also a lake side village of Rara in the northern side. This park was established in 1976. It is the home to musk deer, ghoral, serow, leopard, porcupine, black bear, yellow-throated marten, wilddog, jackles and many kinds of pheasants.

The park is covered by three or four days trekking north ward from Jumla which is linked by air from Kathmandu. There is a provision of government guest house at the lake for the services of the visitors.

(d) Langtang National Park

This park is gazetted in April 1976 and is located in 1,710 sq. kms. It covers 1710 sq. kms. including Langtang valley and surrounding peaks with altitude between 6,500 m.—1500 m. It has a varied ecology from sub-tropical to mountain/alpine. The vegetation varies from temperate forest at the lower elevations with oak, conifer, sub-alpine region with birch forests and alpine grass and bushes. The wide area is covered by blue pine, fir, hemlock, rhododendron arborea, Nepal's national flower. This park is the largest National Park of Nepal and its location is in the central Himalayan region. It is thirty kilometers straight north of Kathmandu. There are some 1,000 plant species, 160 bird species, and 30 mammal species in the park area. It is the home of wild boar, leopard, Himalayan black bear and ghoral, in the lower elevation Himalayan tahr, musk deer, snow leopard, Himalayan black bear in the alpine and sub-alpine regions. Bird species are noticed in the park area which consists of Impeyan pheasants, kaliz pheasants, chukor and grey partridge.

This park is reached by bus or taxi to Trisuli and after that by bus or truck to the Park Headquarter in Dhunche. Lodges run by Government are available at Ghora Tabela and Kyangin and many lodges are managed by private persons all along the trekking route of the Langtang valley. This park is really a glorious botanic and zoological panorama.

(e) Khaptad National Park

Khaptad is situated on Khaptad Lekh having 1850 m. to 3050 m. in altitude and a representative ecology of the middle hills of Nepal. It covers 255 km. It is a rolling plateau of grasslands mixed with forests. This is a abode of the Hindu Sage Khaptad Baha and many pious devotees pay visit each year for workship. In the dense forest inhabit a wide variety of fauna such as leopard, Himalayan black bear, wild dog, wild boar, musk deer and Himalayan tahr. It also supports the bird life such as Kaliz and Danfe (Impeyan) pheasants, finches, orioles and cuckoos. A distinct specimen of fowls named as Chakhura available here. It is the home of the medicinal herbs.

This park can be reached by air from Kathmandu up to Dipayal (Doti, 640 m) and three days trekking from there. Similarly, it can be covered by air Kathmandu up to Bajhang (1250 m) and then two days trekking. These is no facilities in the park for accommodation and fooding at present.

(f) The Annapurna Conservation Area Project

This project is undertaking conservation of natural reserves of the Annapurna Area under the supervision of the King Mahendra Trust for Nature Conservation with the technical and financial assistance of the World Wildlife Fund (WWF), USA. The main objective of the project is to channelize the local community and the local resources for the preservation of natural heritage.

This area surrounds the entire Annapurna range and foothills. This area is full of most spectacular penorama of hamlets in a romantic setting of hill and dale. But this area has to bear increasing stress due to growth of trekkers and enlargement of local population during the last decades. This project is engaged to ensure safe-guarding conservation of natural and cultural resources of the area utilising fees collected from visitors and local sources.

The Annapurna conservation Area project has been recently started with a view to promoting and managing tourism in Annapurna area for proper utilization and management of the natural resources of the region. This area is famous for spectacular mountains, breadth-taking Kali Gandaki rivers, lush rhododendron forests and a rich variety of birds and mammals including the Himalayan Monal pheasant Danfe—the national bird of Nepal, musk-deer and red pands, blue sheep, serow, Himalayan Thar and snow-leopard are all unique attraction of this area.

With the aid of the World Wildlife Fund (WWF) Nepal has launched a project to protect a 2,600 sq. km. area around the Annapurna by ploughing back trekking revenue directly into local conservation efforts. Nepal is Trying hard to conserve natural resources and proper management of all of them. The priority being placed upon conservation in Nepal as this indicates the effect of tourism potential on national park development. Wildlife as a national resource and of tourism is considering as a profitable source of income of foreign currency. But proper care is placed in this project for special ecological problems and measures worked out to check them by the expanded visitation by the tourists. The economic goals of tourism is properly adjusted to the ecological and biological dictates for managing in right direction. This area is becoming very popular among international visitors.

The Annapurna area offers paradise for trekking. Many trekkers trek these areas as they unfold new delights and thrills. Here is where mountain terrain combines with a natural wonderland. Here too, trekkers can see and enjoy such wonders as deepest gorges, snowy peaks, glacier moraines, water falls, rocky as well as green mountain, wildlife and flora and a host of other famous places and sights.

(g) Makalo-Barun National Park and Conservation Area

This park covers Eastern Himalayas and it is 1500 sq. km. It is the first national park, however, to include a zone of strict nature reserve. It is in the Arun Valley which is regarded as one of the world's deepest and picturesque valley. Its location is in the 26°50 to 27°50 N'latitude covering ample area of Mount Makalu I (8463 m), the fifth highest peak in the world and its many other attractive peaks. The valley actually envelops three districts Dhankuta, Bhojpur and Sankhuwasabha in Kosi Zone in Eastern Nepal. Here the Arun river and its tributaries such as Banin, Lekhuwa, Apsuwa, Sankhuwa, Pikhuwa, Induwa, Num and other smaller rivulets flow out the forested valley stretching from the Barun glacier, *i.e.*, west of the Khumbu Himal to the fence of the Khumbhakarna Himal, dominated by Mount Makalu I. In actual meaning, the Makalu-Barun Valley wraps up Sankhuwasabha and Solu Khumbu districts in East Nepal and this area is represented as the Makalu-Barun National Park and Conservation Area. The topography and ecology of the Makalu-Barun National Park and Conservation Area has a diverse eco-systems ranging from snowy peaks to humid sub-tropical rain forests. Vegetations most favourite to this area make up of oak, maple, magnolia, fir, juniper rhododendrons and various herbs. These are more than 45 species of mammals including red panda (a raccoon-like animal, resembling a large domestic cat) musk deer, ghoral, thar, leopard, even snow leopard, serow, barking deer, Himalayan black bear, wild boar etc. Regarding avifauna, these are 200 species in this park. This conservation area is the first model National Park in Nepal which arranges under a fully controlled natural resources management under strict vigilence and the people dwelling near and inside the national park inhabit in conformity with nature. The management is undertaking measures to preserve and protect not only the wilderness and wildlife habitats but also the cultural resources of the ethnic people living in this area through their active participation in development works and resource utilization. It is rich in wide variety of recreational wealth in the mid-lands such as wildlife, fishing, mountain, steams, scenic lakes and excellent climate.

2. Central Region : The mountain region or the central region is formed by the Mahabharat range that soars upto 4877 m and central hills and valleys. To the south of it, Churia foothills lean whose altitude varies from 610 to 1524 m. These two ranges cover between them valleys of different width and altitude from 610 to 914 m. They are called as Inner Terai. The mountain region known as "Pahar" accounts for about 68 percent of the total land area. This region has a sub-tropical and temperate climate two principal hill ranges demarcate their central region from the Terai the Siwalik mountain range in the south and the Mahabharat range to the north. In this region, there are two most fertile and wide valleys namely the Kathmandu and the Pokhara Valley.

This region and the Alpine zone together have four kinds of willows, eight species of evergreen oaks, eleven rhododendrons and a dozon conifers besides birch, alder, hornbean, elm, poplar and valuable walnut. Many other common species include castanopses, Magnolia, Michelia Champaca, Boehmena nigulosa and many others. This region has also a richer fauna. The fauna includes the leopard, the showy clouded leopard, the tiger civet and the rare golden cat other animals are represented by Jackels, wild dog, squirrels, porcupine, mongoose, monkey and ghoral. There are begoni daises dauras hibiscus marigold, violets and a great variety of orchids especially in the valley of Kathmandu and Pokhara.

Among the birds of this region may be mentioned the chir and kalij pheasants, black partridge, while various kinds of pigeon, snipe and occassional duck are seen in the valley of Kathmandu and Pokhara.

The Kathmandu valley is a circular valley and is situated at an altitude of 1330 m. It is encircled by well-wooded hills, Pulchoki in the south-east part (2,800 m), Shivapuri in north (2,713 m), Champa Devi—south-west (2,250 m), close to the Kathmandu city, these are Swayambhu hill, Shivapuri and Nagarjuna (1,989 m) hills. Pokhara valley is also a round basin and its altitude is 950 m. Pokhara valley consists of virgin forest and carpet like meadow in nature's most picturesque setting. Angling is one of the best sports in Pokhara. There are many kinds of fishes in the cold water of the lakes and snow fed rivers. There two valleys are more or less have the same type of flora and fauna. The vegetations represent by patches of pine forests, chir tree, bottle burish, silky oaks, eucalyptus, koiralo and pinus rox burgis etc. The animals inhabit by the Rhesus monkeys, leopard, white hare, rabbits, Jackis squirrels, flying foxes and deers. Birds are dominated by pheasants, jungle fowls, pigeon, vulture, kites, snipe and parrots.

3. **Terai Region** : The lower region or terai region includes southern lowland and Churia (Siwalik) foothills up to about 610 to 1524 m. altutude. This region, which has a width of about 26 to 32 km. and an altitude of maximum 305 m, occupies nearly 17 percent of the total land area of the country. The Eastern Terai is wider and extends continuously while the western Terai is narrower and irregular. The famous forest of the Char-Koshe Jhadi, reknown for big game shootings, lies east to west. It is named after the guess that its average width is 4 kosh (13 km).

This region is known internationally and it has always been famous as a haven to the lover of wild animal and bird life. In order to prevent the extinction and deterioration of rare species of flora and fauna. His Majesty's Government of Nepal has established National Parks and wildlife Reserves (Covering a total area of 7 percent of the country's land area) where hunting and poaching strictly prohibited and where many steps are being taken for the preservation of animals and vegetation in their natural surroundings. A description of National Parks and wildlife reserves is given below:

1. Royal Chitwan National Park

This National Park extends to 932 sq. kms. and lies in the Terai (sub-tropical lowland) an area of riverine grassland and swamp. It is officially gazetted in 1973 as National Park and it is the first national park of the country—Once, in a Rana oligarcy, area for big game shooting and a hunting reserve for the ruling

Rana family for 104 years. The park extends up to the main parts of the Churia Hills and valleys of Rapti, Narayani and Reu rivers. It is extended to the present size in 1977.

This lowland valley of Rapti is famous as the place of protection for one horned rhinoceros. It is regarded as the second largest protected sanctuary of great one-horned rhinoceros in the world. This valley and the rugged Churia hills, sal forests, grasslands and riverine forests including swamps and lakes make ideal place to live for rich variety of large mammals. It is also famous for tiger population. About 300 varieties of birds are noticed in this park. It is rich with such fauna as tiger, leopard, gaur, sloth bear, sambar, Chital, hog deer, barking deer, wild boar, fresh water dolphin and crocodiles.

This national park is fully developed with all sort of facilities for an wildlife adventure in the Himalayan foothills and jungle. It is famous for Tiger Tops Jungle Lodge-'tree top' hotel with all modern facilites in the rustic comfort of the jungle. There are many other safari lodges and tented camps for the visitors.

Getting to this park is easy. There is air service from Kathmandu in the Chitwan valley, approximately 75 miles south west of Kathmandu (flight time 30 minutes only). There is provision of all kinds of safari-viewing wildlife through elephant ride, boating, nature walks, river rafting, short trek through forest and hills, camping landrover excursions and fishing. All these wild life safari are conducted by an experienced guide and so the visitor will get the chance always to see stampeding great one horned Rhinoceros, stately tiger and other species of animals. It is a park nominated to the World Heritage list in 1984 by the World Heritage Committee. This park is easily reached by road, air or on a raft down the Trisuli and Narayani rivers.

2. Royal Bardia National Park

This is the national park recently upgraded from a wildlife reserve. It is 368 sq. km. and is situated in the mid-west Terai in the river bed of the Karnali and the Babai in Bardiya district. It was once also a Royal Shikar Reserve, now it contains the surviving population of tiger in Nepal. This area of Sal forest has been given special recognition by the World Wildlife Fund's "Operation Tiger" project.

The feature of this park covers north and east part by the foothill of the Siwalik Hills which goes steeply to the plains in the south. This park is full of Sal forest and with tropical semi-deciduous vegetations. It is the home of tiger, leopard, blue bull, samber, spotted deer, wild boar etc. It is noted for crocodiles and gangatic dolphin. The river is also rich for its masheer fish. Many kinds of birdlife are found in the park. The Karnali Tented Camp is there on the banks of the Karnali river. Wildlife viewing can be enjoyed through elephant's back.

Access to this park is by flight by air or by road to Nepalgunj and then about is hours by vehicle to the park headquarters. This park is of interest for ungulates and tiger.

WILDLIFE RESERVES

Suklaphanta Wildlife Reserve

This reserve is located in the south-west corner of Nepal in the riverine belt of the Mahakali river. It covers an area of 305 square kilometers of grassland, sal forest, Khair and sissoo forest and mixed deciduous forest. Some measures for the protection of wildlife in this area had been taken since 1965 but it was gazetted as a wildlife reserve in 1976.

This open grassland area and forest in the western Terai includes tiger, leopard, bear, sambhar, chital, hog deer and nilgai (blue bull). This is of special interest for swamp deer (cervus duvavceli) and this reserve has got a large population of it. Other ungulates include the spotted deer and wild boar. There are also few wild elephants are noticed here. There are number of migrating and nature birds in this area. This open wide grassy land covered with dense forest in between and swamp is best for game viewing. There is a small lake known as Rani Tal which are full of water-fowls of all kinds. Some of the migratory birds are also noticed in this lake at certain season.

Koshi Tappu Wildlife Reserve

This reserve is situated on the banks of the Kosi river in the eastern Terai. It is 175 sq. km. and the reverine flood plains of the Kosi river. This is the habitat of the last of the Asiatic Wild Buffalo (Bubalus bubalus) in Nepal. These buffalos live in the narrow belt of 4-6 km. of wet grassland and reverine forest of Sal in the Kosi embankments.

This reserve lies 57 km. west of Biratnagar, Nepal's industrial city. There are number of ponds and many colourful birds are seen in their eating fishes. Many migratory waterfalls have been throng near the barrage making it as one of the Nepal's best place for bird watching. This is also a excellent areas for aquatic avi-fauna.

Being the floodplain of the Saptakoshi river, the vegetations consists of tall grass, Khair, Sissou and mixed deciduous forest. There are also a population of hog deer and wild boars. Some spotted deer and blue-bull as also noticed here.

Bird-watching from selected vantage points best opportunity to spot many of migrating birds and resident game birds. Some of the birds are likely to view well be among the may species of egrets, comorants, kingfishers, parrakeets, owls, eagles, stroks, the rarer paradise flycatcher, scarlet minivet and kites. Migratory and ducks and gooses are also noticed in the mudflats. This reserve is regarded as the location in the major migration direction of the birds from the North.

Parsa Reserve (499 sq. kms.)

This wildlife reserve lies to the east of Royal Chitwan National Park. It was famous for big game hunting. The actual landscape of the reserve are the Churia Hills running east to west. The forest is 'Sal' dominant, chir, pine grow in the Churia hills and along the rivers.

The reserve shelters some of Asia's richest wildlife population wild elephant, tiger, leopard, sloth bear, gaur, blue ratel, palm civet and jungle cat.

Different species of birds like peacock, jungle fowl, black partridge and geese on the pools and great rivers.

This reserve is easily accessible from Kathmandu. It is connected by Kathmandu Birgunj highway. It is also connected by air by Kathmandu to Simra.

There is facilities of guest house and lodges. It is better to pre-arrange from Kathmandu for food and shelter.

Hunting

Nepal is one of the best hunting grounds in the world. The dense jungles of Terai are full of game animals such as Tigers, leopards, panthers, hyena, nilgai, serow, marten, bears, spotted deer, wild boars, wild buffalows, ghral, wolves etc. Many kinds of bird life like kaliz, black partridge, peacocks, jungle fowls, magpie are also found. Other birds are lophophorus, chyakhura pigeon, valture, kites, snipe, duck, parrots, muniya etc. In the Himalayan side musk-deer, white bears are also noticed. Nepal once renowned for its abundance and variety of big game, now has lost natural habitat of much of its flora and fauna due to population explosion and their settlements causing loss to virgin forests. In order to check the damage of its natural heritage, Nepal has launched conservation and management of this important zoo-geography of the earth. Many national parks and wildlife reserves have been designated in various parks of the country and protection has been given to many of the country's flora and fauna. These measures have also checked deforestation and environmental degradation. Big game shooting is not granted in Nepal simply because of destroyed natural habitat of fauna and their extention. However, a controlled hunting is permitted in some parts by paying fees.

Dhorpatan Hunting Reserve

This reserve is situated in Baglung district in the Dhaulagiri

Himalayan region in Western Nepal. It covers an area of 1325 sq. km. The feature of this reserve is that many species of vegetations of alpine climate are found in the north and mixed hard wood at lower elevations. The plain area is rich in many kinds of vegetations such as fir, pine, birch, rhododendron, hemlock, oaks, Junipers and spruce. This is one of the prime habitants of blue sheep other game animals are ghoral, serow, Himalayan Thar, Himalaya black bear, barking deer, pheasants and partridges. Endangered species include in this reserve red panda and cheer pheasant. A controlled hunting is permitted. This reserve offers world calss sport for blue sheep.

Honey Hunting

This honey hunting sport is not developed in Nepal so far, but it is considered that it has got the biggest scope. There are so many areas in Nepal where bee lives are plentiful and this hunting sport can be arranged in the proper season.

Nepal is a botanist and zoologist paradise. Despite human incursions due to population growth and the need for agricultural lands, Nepal continues to have some of the most beautiful flora and fauna in the world. The temperature, climate and rainfall vary from place to place. The country is greatly influenced by the topography and the flora and fauna with the difference in the climatic conditions and the range of altitudes. The most spectacular wildlife lies in the tropical Terai belt in which the Chitwan National Park is located. However, the mountain and alpine areas also have potential national parks for viewing wildlife. A number of National Park, wildlife reserves and hunting reserve have been designated in a completely unspoilt wilderness to project diminishing woldlife for coming generations to see and to observe as a last species of world natural heritage.

Natural panorama and beauty of the natural surrounding are considered the raw material for tourism. Due to its physiographical frame, Nepal unfolds natural and scenic attractions of singular diffusion extending from the tropical forest belt in the south to the lofty alpine regions and the herein landscape of the plateau, intervening these limits spread areas plenty of outermost scenic landscape fastening a sumptuous diversified possession of recreational resources. It is this usual feature which forms some of earth's most impressive tourist attractions. The sublime mountain loops of the Himalayas are an enticement not only for world's alpinists but also exhibit an important asset to recreational use and an essential facet to cultural tourism.

Wildlife resources of the Terai plains and in the various regions of the country represent potential suitable for adventure tourism. A rich wildlife and other valuable assets to recreational use are the country's natural forests, snow-fed rivers and lakes providing recreational activities such as white water rafting, fishing, boating and wild life watching.

The prospects for adventure tourism are greater in Nepal where altitude topography and climate stipulate ideal pre-requisites for such activities. Nepal has got four valuable assets for the development of adventure tourism and these are pointed out in this chapter. All operations for adventure tourism are manned and managed by the licensed travel and trekking agencies who sell, rent and arrange everything a visitor needs. Nepal is a holiday kingdom with a series of adventure tours with different duration and thrill.

7

BUSINESS TOURISM

Business Tourism to Nepal is increasing. The international tourist movement is concentrated in bigger and bigger numbers towards Nepal which has only in the last two decades or so appeared on the world tourist market.

Nepal envelopes a variety of climate and geographical features and, on the other hand, a national culture of great value. Nepal has therefore, continually exercised an increasing attraction on business tourism. It is touristically attractive and has become willingly visited by tourists of all forms as it ensures that it is suitably and easily accessible. The phenomenon corresponds to an increasing, broadening of the market from which it profits.

Business tourism implies as elsewhere, in Nepal not only the professional journeys of businessmen or industrialists but all journeys which have as their purpose of visit to fairs and exhibitions, or of technical achievements which broden a rather general interest among people who have nothing in common with the profession in question. Business can prompt a person to make a journey for tourist reasons as well. The diversity of touristic motivations is equivalent to the diversity of the types of tourism which, at present can be enjoyed in the world. In other respects, it should not be forgotten that businessmen behave not only as consumers, but often during their free time, as real tourists by profiting from the distractions offered by the country.

The business travel constitutes major expenditure of business, but the business tourist consumption includes spending on transport, expenditure in hotels, restaurants, cafes, spendings on sightseeing, entertainment and purchase of souvenirs. So the business tourism consumption, actually, in Nepal represents the whole of the expenditure of all, regardless of purpose of visit business.

Nepal is regarded as one of the poor industrialized countries of the world. No doubt, modern industrial development to Nepal began in1936. Thereafter, a scroll of industries emerged and are still operating. Industries in Nepal are divided into four categories: Cottage, small, medium and large. The major large scale and small scale industries of Nepal are sugar, cigarettes, agriculture tools, bricks, textiles, leather and shoe, drugs, marbles, cement, tea jute etc. Cottage industries based on animal products, geological products and forest products are also operating in Nepal.

Nepal is one of the least developed countries of the world. Its per capita income is estimated to be US$140. It has adopted a mixed economy which is divided into the private, Government and the public sector. It is predominantly an agricultural country. Tourism has now taken a quantitative place in a country economy. Tourism is composed of very varied consumption, sightseeing, meals, drinks, entertainment. It also helps to increase the employment and related enterprises. So the economic value of tourism is immense.

The role of tourism in the economy of the country has shown that it has already ascertained a very leading place. Tourism is regarded as an industry and encouragement is given to the private sector to come up in establishing various tourist service industries. Tourism industry, as such, had developed since 1960 and the public and private sectors equally had shared in the development. It has been accorded high priority in the development plan of Nepal. It has not only extensively contributd to foreign exchange earnings in the country but also prominently expanded its impact on various sectors of the economy. The spectacular growth of international tourists has been accelerated in the country in the past decades. It has helped much for the development of arts and crafts and much for the development of arts and crafts and providing employment to many persons on this trade. Nepali handicraft are very famous smong the international visitors as souvenirs. Nepal's traditional artistic skill are best demonstrated on the bronze sculptures, wood and stone carvings, khukris (gorkha knives), Grassware and religious artifacts. The smooth pashmina showls and clothing and Tibetan handicraft such as satchels and belts are equally famous.

Nepal is one of the best countries in the orient for the purchase of good souvenirs. The different varieties of souvenirs are very real and reflect the ancient traditions. Variety of souvenirs constitute a rare ensemble of replica of an ancient architecture and delicate artifacts of great originality and quality. There are different varieties of souvenirs. They, cover in some ways, the following items, *i.e.* miniature replicas such as images of Gods and Goddesses with carved work in wood, metal and ivory; traditional handicraft, silver ornaments, jewellery studded with semi-preceous stones, herbs, potteries, ceramics and others. Equally popular among the international tourists is hand knotted wollen carpets, readymade garments and leather goods. Good buys are also Thankas of different sizes and colours full of treasured art forms in the eloquent paintings on Buddhism.

Shopping can be very rewarding and exciting in Nepal specially in the tri-cities, Kathmandu, Patan and Bhadgaon and Pokhara. There are numerous and varied shops lined on the main streets and in the arcades of hotels—cottage industry and handicraft production form one of the regular features of Nepali life. Cottage industry is based solely on indigenous labour and local resources. Handicraft are considered to the one of the large part of Nepali export items. All these artistic handicraft are made by hand according to the process handed down from generation to generation. These artifacts are very good in craftsmanship and are good for antiques. The range of handicrafts, in general, consist of sculpture in detail bronze casting of idols and other figures and wood carvings with exquisite designs. Nearly 94 percent of the working population in Nepal are dependent upon agriculture that produces about 60 per cent GDP. His Majesty's Government mobilises national as well as local resources for development whereas public sector comprises basic industries. The private sector covers the rest of the economy corresponding with the main strategy for economic development. The trade policy of Nepal has also been liberalised in recent years. The aim of the new policy approach is to furnish Nepalese producers with better incentives for both external and internal trade. Side by side with liberal policy of trade, Nepal has opened the doors to foreign investment. Now foreign investment projects and many technical collaboration projects have been registered in Nepal. The foreign investment have accommodated from India, U.S.A. Switzerland, Federal Republic of Germany, Japan, China, U.K. and from other countries. Technical collaboration projects have accorded mostly from India, Japan South Korea, China, USA and Hongkong. The investments are garnered up in garments minerals, chemicals, tourist hotels and restaurants plus specialized services and food and beverage industries. The technical collaboration agreements are generally in electronics, chemicals and food and beverage divisions. So Nepal is assured of profitable investment and has a favourable environment for business tourism due to attractive investment incentives and warm and hospitable people.

Nepal now becoming a strategic location for foreign investment. Since the re-instalating of parliamentary system of Government in 1990, Nepal has been followed gushing and outward economic policies bestowing greater importane to the private sector. The liberalisation policy breaking the ice in 1991 with important structural reforms in fiscal, monetary, industrial, commercial and labour policies has wedged leading emphasis on industrial development with ample incentives and facilities to the local as well as foreign investors. The Industrial Policy (IP) and Foreign Investment and One Window Policy (FIOWP) harmonizing enactments has been clear making the government to assists with the role of promoting and assisting the investors. The Industrial policy revised in 1992 has identified the industries under different categories. At the same time it has made a provisions to protect and provided a good gesture to the foreign investors to open industries in Nepal.

Nepal now needs Travel Industry Development Program. The measure of bringing professional and financial assistance to provisions in formulating tourism development plans. This is fundamental to the tourism program. So Nepal must now move forward for bringing selective technical and financial assistance from the touristically advanced countries of the world for the development for critically needed facilites and attractions. This sort of assistance will surely help to improve productivity and management standards of private tourism operators and so facilitate access to sources of capital. This includes for example technological improvement program. Production of carpets were organised in three areas Jawalakhel, Hyangza, Chialsa under one factory system in 1960. Increasing number of manufacturing carpets were established by private investors and a ever growing number of importers, namely from European countries started placing manufacturing orders in large quantities, causing boom to the present day high position of this industry in Nepal.

There are many kinds of carpets available in Nepal and of different styles and using different craft and dyes. But whatever, their designs and decors, all carpets are made of knotted wool. The best carpets are made from pure Tibetan or a mix of Tibetan and New Zealand wools and the best yarn is handspun. Usually fine carpets have 48 or 60 kpsi and 100 knots per square inch carpets are expensive. There are also variety of styles. Traditional Tibetan carpet is bright in colours and bold in design, neo-Tibetan consisted of undyed wool in pastel colours and traditional decorations, modern with pastel colours and designed with floral or abstract motifs. Dyes are of two types—chemical and vegetable. The carpet made of using chemical dyes are bright and fast in colour. The chemical is usually used with high quality European ingrediants. The carpet produced by using vegetable dyes is not fast in colour.

The Nepal manufactures have now introduced design and

colours in line with the present day market taste while in close collaboration with the European Importers. There are now a wide range of sizes, replacing the traditional Tibetan size of 3x6 ft. The largest size, however, comprise of 15x20 ft.

The carpet is produced based on the ancient methods. Hand processing is used throughout the production. Carpets manufactured in Nepal are more detailed, have a lower file and are more dense and substantial, resulting from the closer tighter weave. The quality and price differ on the type of wool used (Tibetan or blend), dye, density of knots, thickness of the gange rod used and the traditional design. Colours are of different kinds brilliant red and blues to dusty roses lavender, signifying the chemical and vegetables dyes by brilliance and dusty. Carpets have become the leading export items of Nepal to other countries. Being one of the largest industry in the country, the carpet industry not only earns valuable foreign exchange but also provides livelihood for many people. Carpets made in Dharchula, a district situated in far western region of Nepal are very plain but excellent. Dharchula is one of the three main points of entry of Tibetan wool into Nepal.

The major carpet import countries of Nepal are Austria, Belgium, France, Germany Ireland, Switzerland, Sweden, the Netherlands, United Kingdom and U.S.A. Germany is the dominant country taking more then 80 per cent of the local export share.

Readymade Garments

Nepal is now also popular for the export of her variety of readymade garments. Many readymade garment industries have been established in Kathmandu valley and they are producing a large number of readymade outfits for export. Readymade garments are good, inexpensible and fashionable. The textiles used for the production of readymade garments are cotton, silk and wollen materials. There garments are of high quality textiles and of standard design to meet the modern taste of fashion quality for perfection and proportion. Souvenirs in Nepal in any form replicas of architecture, painting or carvings on stone, wood or metal are at their best conform and flowing. They are primarily rhythmic and plastic. They are spontaneous, elaborate in design and exhilerating. The conception and overall representation are wholly traditional but they are embellished with a daring richness of details and a delicate touch of workmanship.

The following description are some of the many items of attractive souvenirs available in the shops of cities in Nepal.

Miniature Replicas of Ancient Arts and Architecture

Nepal is known for its artistic reproductions of miniatures of ancient arts and architectures as statuettes of Gods and Goddesses with minute details, as well as the model of age-old architectures, the doors and windows of the anceint palaces in wood, metal and ivory. These art objects consists of figures of various gods and goddesses, birds, animals or miniature replicas of ancient architecture. The artistic designs in all the art objects or replicas are well executed and carved by hand with high skill. These art objects are created out of the techniques handed down through the by-gone ages and generations. The artisans still give their energy and time as in ancient times to create art objects displaying a devotion of craft and an instinctive feeling for beauty and grace. These art objects form the traditional handicrafts of Nepal. Active handicrafts, bronze and brass in Patan, pottery in Themi, wood-carving and painting testifies that the traditional taste is still living. There are also variety of folkcrafts which are amongst the most eagerly sought products. In addition, there are costume jewellery set with silver jade and other simi-precious stones. Nepali handicraft items are many and varied such as fignee work decorated with precious and semi-precious stones, pottery consisting of clay pots, flower vases, candle stems, ashtrays and masks, wood carving portraying intricate carried window frames, door frames latticed window and temple supports. Many kinds of potteries as well as household goods and decorations made out of ceramics are of superb design and outlook. Basket works are generally made of reed, bamboo and variety of forest grasses. Many kinds of baskets bag and decorative items are artistic and good for uses. Such items of basket works made in Dang, Ghorahi, Nepalgunj and Lumbini are excellent.

Hand Knotted Woollen Carpets

Nepal is popular since time immemorial for its wool. But the production of hand knotted wollen carpets has increased over the recent years with the coming of Tibetan refugees into Kathmandu. Tibetan carpets made in Nepal are the country's number one export at present. These carpets are produced in Nepal by the traditional Tibetan technique. The production of carpets started in the year 1960 with a view to cope with commercial demands. The carpet making process was developed for the first time around 1960 under an agreement between the His Majesty's Government of Nepal and Federal Government of Switzerland with technical co-operation providing financial, technical and marketing assistance for the same. Pashmina and woolen garments are the finest. Nepal is known the world over for high standard for making the forest Pashmina rugs, shawls and scarfs. These rugs, shawls and scarfs are made of finest wool sheared out of the Himalayan goats and sheeps on the traditional handlooms.

Along with ready made garments, Pashmina and wollen garments, cloth-made shoes and slippers are also popular as seminars. The material used for making cloth-made shoes and shippers are velvet and wool and the sole is usually made of thick knotted threads. These shoes and slippers are in great demand for use as bed room slippers. The more prised varieties have embroidery designs.

National cap of Nepal is equally popular among the visitor. The national headness is of two types. One is of black colour and is popular as Bhadgauli Topi as this cap was firstly made in the city of Bhadgaon. Caps of printed muslim are also available. Many pointed cap is also available and there are attractive in the simplicity of its style and beauty. Tansen and Terhathum districts of Nepal produce five Dhaka Shawls which are famous in beauty and decor.

Paper-mache Masks and Dolls

Nepali Masks are of many designs depicted on elaborate techniques of dying and art-features with different looks artistically modelled to represent the Hindu pantheon. Their attraction lies in their intricate, gorgeous designs casted with various colours on the outer surface.

Side by side with paper-mache masks, dolls in authentic Nepalese costumes of all sizes and models are available. Dolls are dressed in simple and gorgeous costumes. They look like life-like and represent the Nepali way of life. They provide education along with entertainment.

Metal Products

Metal products cover different art objects such as powder case, make-up boxes, ashtrays, flower vases, silver and brass utensils, picture frames etc. they envelope traditional taste with modern designs for use as decorative objects etc. There are also a number of costume jewellery and there are decorated with semi-previous stones such as ruby, Aquamarine cat's eye, coral tourmaline and jade.

Most famous metal product is Khukuri-curved national weapon of Nepal. Khukuri is made of iron and is the representation of Nepali bravery and chivalry. The handle and scabbard of this weapon are usually carved with symbolic figures in ivory or metal on top of cloth casting. The Nepali craftsman attach great importance for the manufacturing of this national knife with good metal in order to maintain world-wide reputation intact.

Thankas or Paubhas

Nepali Thankas or scroll paintings are very popular among the international visitors. Most of the Thankas depict objects and scenes derived from the Hindu and Buddhist mythologies. Thankas are brocade paintings supported by a thick white cotton textile. They can be easily rolled up to form a scroll.

The objects are outlined by the traditional line drawing. The pigments used for making painting on the Thankas are made locally. The costly Thanka is painted with a lavish use of real gold ink. Most famous amongst the traditional paintings are Thankas and Paubhas which come in different sizes though the shape is normally square or rectangular.

Shopping and souvenir hunting in Kathmandu, Patan, Bhadgaon and Boudhnath are worth visiting. Many art objects are just as likely to come across an age-old treasure or family collection as well as samples of Nepali and Tibetan artifacts made more recently but in the time—honoured tradition handed down from generation to generation.

The Tibetans objects to be noticed in Boudhnath, the many shops in Kathmandu and the Tibetan Refugee Centre, Jawalakhel, Patan include prayer-wheels of wood, ivory, silver or copper, belt buckles, jewellery, bowls, ceremonial articles of religious interest like the thunder-bolts, water vessels, charms boxes, rosary beads, musical instruments, such as trumpets, gongs, small drums and the secred conch shell horn, hand-woven carpets. Tibetan style jackets, dresses broaded furtrimmed hats and bags. Bhadgaon is still the site of a weaving and pottery industry. Ancient forms and designs are preserved as souvenirs and can be purchased wandering round the city. Actually, visitors have a choice of many gifts and presents all over Nepal.

Kathmandu is now fast growing as venue for international meets and it has holding a very practical aspect for the growth of business tourism. Many regional and international seminars, conferences and workshops are fast growing in Kathmandu and the convention tourism from India as well as from other countries are also contributing greatly to the promotion of business tourism. Indian industrialists are now making choices of Nepal for making series for their general meetings of the industries.

Nepal is a land of cultural past which is enshrined in many magnificent monument and work of art. Her proud tradition of craftsmanship dates back to thousands of years. Many craftsman in the country live and toil to preserve and enrich long tradition. The handicrafts of Nepal, therefore, reflect of vigorous and thriving tradition that has come down unbroken through the ages. So Nepal offers good opportunity for business travel as she has many items of export for transactions.

The typical traditional souvenirs include Thankas, filignee works, wood carving, pashmina shawls, Gorkha knives, paper masks, lamp shades, bronze statuette, traditional silver jewellery, jewellery studded with simi-precious jewels.

Thamel keeps many good souvenirs for the visitors. Visitors can get almost every item of souvenirs typical of the country right here. It is a tourist rendezvous.

Nepal is enshrined in many a magnificent monuments and works of art with a civilization stretching back to thousand of years before the birth o Christ, with a culture richly endowed by the fusion of two of the truly great religions of mankind, Hinduism and Buddhism and with an unbroken art tradition. Nepal holds a unique place in the tourist map of the world.

Nepalese art is as pre-eminent and impressive as the noble architectural works created by craftsmen during the ancient and medieval periods of Nepal. The high degree of excellence in the world of arts and crafts is expressed by the finest and most luminous pieces of bronze sculpturing, wood and stone carving.

Arts is Nepal in any form architecture, painting or carvings on stone and metal are at their best uniform and flowing. They are primarily rhythmic and plastic. They are spontaneous, elaborate in design and exhilerating. The conception and the overall design are wholly traditional but they are embellished with a daring richness of details and a delicate touch of workmanship.

Along with different variety of items of souvenirs for international visitors, many cultural plant such as indoor and outdoor theatres, libraries, museums, galleries, zoological and botanical gardens, multi-purpose meeting-rooms (for conference, concerts, congresses, etc.) are now constructed and are made ready for international events. So the business tourism implies the professional journeys of businessmen or industrialists to attain conferences or exhibitions and also make a tour of sightseeing places nothing in common with the profession in question. There is plenty of opportunity for the growth of conference tourism with the establishment of convention facilities and it has been gaining more and more importance. Many conferences, assemblies and national symposia which are held from time to time with the attainment for many invites from different countries will surely cause to enhance the development of tourism. Sometime international conferences are also organised. These conferences and meetings cause the attainment of number of participants who generally stay several days in the country. This cause a sufficient occupancy of hotels. So, many countries now aware of the serious economic aspect of conferences, endeavour to construct appropriate premises or even to build 'conference halls' with all necessary modern facilites. So these participants from various country can make a tour as real tourists by enjoying from the attractions offered by the country. So business tourism has a big role to play in the tourism development of a country.

Nepal has now International Convention Centre. This centre is well-equipped with modern facilities to organize big conferences, seminars workshops and trainings. This centre covers an area of 8.5 hectare of with main Convention hall with capacity for 1000 persons. Side by side with this, big hotels have also facilities for Conventions.

8

CONCLUSIONS

The development of tourism in Nepal mirrors the constant growth—high rates of growth are in evidence during recent years. Nepal has now placed high priority on the development of tourism through which development in other sectors of the economy is to be achieved.

International tourism has had considerable impact on Nepal which is not uncommon in view of the smallness of the country and the rapid growth of the tourism industry. There is greater awareness and appreciation of things Nepali, not only cultural heritage such as temples, stupas, historical monuments but also natural heritage, arts and crafts and even locally produced beer. These, in turn have also been affected by tourist tastes and expectations. The Nepal concept of the quality of life has also touched the influence of tourism. This is reflected not only in architectural styles of hotel building but also in the increased popularity among the Nepali urban dwellers of such leisure activities as visits to restaurants and clubs.

The tourist sector initially flourished in the country's marginal areas (Kathmandu Valley, Pokhara, Everest Region and some of the other tourist spots) which are primarily rich in cultural and natural attractions. The construction of tourist infrastructures such as hotels in these areas further accentuated the big concentration of facilities, employment and business. The expansion of employment opportunities is related to fulfil the demand of the hotel industry, travel and trekking agencies as a whole for a range of supporting and ancillary services. Although the number of such establishments has grown tremendously, many of them face difficulty to survive simply due to the seasonal nature and non-permanent nature of the trade and these services are only for tourists. His Majesty's Government of Nepal's policy for granting licences for such organisations and service industry is liberal and many hotels, travel, trekking, rafting, jungle safari agencies are opened to cater the tourists. The demand of job in tourism and lack of trained power to man and manage the industry and the service sector, encourages both intra and inter-regional migration. The extent to which local people will benefit more or less than other from this employment generation depends on many factors. High level jobs go to expatriates to non-availability of trained local staffs. To strike while the iron is hot, tourism research is of urgent need. Research means, as all we know, a careful search or investigation or systematic investigation towards increasing the sum of knowledge. Now tourism research is needed and to he carried out for pin-pointing how far the industry is alive to its own perspective and is especially conscious of its economic benefits and its negative effects and over all significance to the country. The situation in Nepal, as it seems extraordinary in that the demands, constraints, risks and potentials of a fragile agricultural environment, a large urban nucleus, specially in Kathmandu Valley, and emerging housing boom and tourism are surging head on. The service industry, so far, proves to be oriented to servicing foreigners and so more inclines to foreign imports, not realizing the import substitution. With all these effects on the growth of tourism in Nepal, no exploration and study are being made to pin point the specific points such as tourist types , the various stages of tourism development the impact of tourism in socio-cultural affairs and planned versus "Spontaneous" tourism in the country.

It is knwn to all of us that touristic consumption consists of three characteristics, *i.e.*, (1) Transportion payment, (2) payment for boarding and lodging and lastly, (3) payment for touring or sightseeing or appreciation. So will, leisure and shopping lead demand in tourism, tourist facilities and potentials subordinate supply. So the factors of touristic demand must be analysed from time to time in order to find out the macro-economic aspects relating to tourism with the economy and to gause the basis for the role of tourism in economic growth of the country. Review must be done in planning process in Nepal and identified clearly the major interests of both private enterprises and HMG in the development of tourism. So a study may be assessed more accurately by a thorough study of demand (the tourist market) in coordination with private sector such steps have helped to analyse tourist demand with a view to adopting necessary measures for channelling any unexpected tourist flows more efficiently. If such regular study and analysis will be carried out, there is every hope that tourism will be developed more rationally and to the help of the community of the country 2nd enhancing the national economy of the country.

BIBLIOGRAPHY

1. Unknown Nepal—R.N.W. Bishop, Luzac & Company Ltd., London W.C.I., 1952.
2. East of Kathmandu—Tom Weir, Oliver and Boyd, London, 1955.
3. In Highest Nepal—Norman Hardie, George Allen & Unwin Ltd., London, 1957.
4. Guide to Enjoying Nepalese Festivals—Jim Goodman, Asian Printing Press, Kathmandu, 1981.
5. Nepal Namaste—Robert Rieffel, Sahayogi Prakashan, Tripureswar, Kathmandu, 1978.
6. Kathmandu—Simpson, Colin, Angus and Robertson Ltd., 1967, London.
7. Festivals of Nepal—Anderson, Mary M., George Allen and Unwin Ltd., London, 1991.
8. The Kathmandu, Nepal Handbook, Uttaracress and Kesang G. Tseten, Kathmandu, 1983.
9. Pictureseque Nepal—A Handbook for Tourist, Amatya Jagdish Man Singh, Kathmandu, 1956.
10. Fairs & Festivals of Nepal—Tek. B., Khatri, HMG, Ministry of Communication Department of Information, Kathmandu, 1982.
11. A Catalogue on Nepal—Bajracharya Manik Lal, Eastern Trading and Investment Co., Kathmandu, 1973.
12. The Temples of Nepal—Bernier, Ronald, M., Sangam Press, Kathmandu, 1970.

13. Nepal, Land of Mystery—Hassoldt Davis, Robert Hale Limited, London, 1959.

14. History of Nepal—Daniel Wright, M.A.M.D. Cambridge, 1877.

15. An Account of the Kingdom of Nepal—Kirkpatrick W., W. Miller, London, 1811.

16. Nepal Vol. I & II—London Perceval Constable, London, 1928.

17. Sketches From Nepal—Oldfield H.A. Allen & Co., London, 1880.

18. N.M. Bajracharya—Buddhism in Nepal 465 B.C. to 1199 AD, 1998.

19. K.S. Valdiya—Dynamic Himalaya, 1998.

INDEX